Savory Salads

Tupperware welcomes you to the refreshing world of *Savory Salads*. Here you'll find taste-tempting recipes for classics, hearty whole-meal salads, palate-pleasing pasta mixtures, and fresh-fruit platters. To top them off, try one of the flavorful dressings featured in their own special chapter. So go ahead. Start with the star on the cover—Turkey-Strawberry Salad—and enter Tupperware's realm of super salads. Enjoy!

This seal assures you that every recipe in **Savory Salads** has been tested in the *Better Homes and Gardens*® Test Kitchen. This means that each recipe is practical and reliable, and meets high standards of taste appeal.

All microwave tests were completed in a variety of high-wattage microwave ovens. Cooking times are approximate since microwave ovens vary by manufacturer.

Tupperware™

Contents

Creating
Sensational Salads

With the ever-increasing assortment of salad ingredients available, putting together an attractive, delicious salad has become an exciting adventure. The key to success is buying the freshest ingredients possible, then using Tupperware products to make sure they stay market fresh.

Go for the Green

It's important to start with high-quality greens. Always choose fresh-looking heads or bunches and avoid those with shriveled, wilted, or brown leaves. Heads of lettuce should be firm but not hard.

Once you've brought the greens home, wash them well. Start by removing any bruised or tough outer leaves. To clean iceberg lettuce, loosen the core by hitting the stem end sharply on the countertop. Then twist and lift out the core. Wash the lettuce by holding the head, core side up, under cold running water. Rinse the lettuce thoroughly, then invert the head and let it drain well. Place the head in an airtight container, such as the Tupperware® Super Crisp-It® container. To clean leaf lettuce, romaine, Boston lettuce, and curly endive, cut off the bottom core and wash the leaves under cold running water. Then drain them in a colander, such as the Tupperware double colander features.

Keep Them Crisp

Drain the greens well because excess water causes stored greens to deteriorate more quickly. It also dilutes the flavor of salad dressings and makes salads soggy. After draining, place the greens on a clean kitchen towel or on several layers of paper towels. Place a second towel or more paper towels over the greens and gently pat them dry.

Wrap the dried greens in a dry kitchen towel or paper towels and refrigerate them for at least 30 minutes. If you're not planning to use the greens right away, place them in an airtight container. Or, unwrap and store the greens in the Tupperware Produce Manager™ container. To use the greens, tear them into bite-size pieces.

Dressing Dos

For light and fluffy tossed salads, place the torn greens and other salad ingredients in a bowl large enough to allow plenty of room for tossing. The Tupperware Celebration Series bowl or any other large Tupperware bowl works well for this. To keep the salad crisp, add the dressing just before serving and add only enough to lightly coat the leaves. Toss the salad with salad servers or the Tupperware Celebration Series Servers. Gently push downward to the bottom of the bowl and lift up and over.

When it comes to arranged salads, use your creative flair. Design the salad in any way pleasing to your eye. Start with a bed of greens, if you like. Arrange them on individual plates or use a single large platter or tray, like the oval tray from the Tupperware Watercolor® Hors D'oeuvre set. Then add the larger ingredients and top the salad with the more delicate items.

For marinated salads, start by placing the items to be marinated in a dish or the Tupperware Season-Serve® container. Then pour the marinade over the food. Cover the dish or apply the seal to the Season-Serve container. Refrigerate the salad for as long as directed in your recipe. Be sure to stir the salad or invert the Season-Serve container several times to distribute the marinade.

Garnishes Galore

For a touch of sophistication, garnish your salads with fresh herbs or edible flowers.

Fresh Herbs: Add sprigs of herbs, such as tarragon, dill, thyme, cilantro, or rosemary for that just-right accent. Or, toss herbs together with greens for an interesting blend of flavors.

Edible Flowers: The flowers best suited for salads are chive blossoms, nasturtiums, pansies, rose petals, calendulas, marigolds, borage, dianthus, daylilies, and geraniums. Be sure to use only these flowers or others you know to be safe. Use unsprayed blossoms from your garden, the supermarket produce section, or a restaurant or produce supplier. Make sure that the flowers were grown without the use of pesticides or other chemicals. Avoid flowers from florist shops. They're usually treated with chemicals.

Salad Greens Identification

Watercress
Small, round, delicate leaves on edible stems; peppery flavor.

Curly endive (chicory)
Frilly, narrow, prickly leaves with a pleasantly bitter tang. Baby curly endive has a softer texture than the mature form.

Escarole
Broad, irregularly shaped, flat leaves with slightly curled edges; firm, chewy texture with mildly bitter flavor.

Butterhead lettuce
Small, loosely packed leaves; subtly sweet, buttery flavor. Boston and Bibb lettuce are butterhead varieties. Bibb lettuce is slightly darker and has a smaller head than Boston lettuce. Red-tip butterhead also is available.

Salad savoy (flowering kale)
Large frilly leaves that can be purple, pink, green, or creamy white; cabbagelike flavor.

Belgian endive
Long, slender, creamy white leaves with pale yellow tips; slightly bitter flavor. Red-tip Belgian endive also is available.

Watercress

Curly endive

Escarole

Butterhead lettuce

Salad savoy

Belgian endive

Mesclun
Mixture of piquant and delicate baby lettuces grown in rows next to each other and harvested at the same time. The lettuce varieties in mesclun depend on the season, but they always include a combination of flavors, texture, and colors.

Radicchio
Ruby-red leaves with thick, white veins that form a small, round, compact head; bitter and peppery tasting.

Arugula
Small, slender leaves similar in appearance to dandelion greens; a pungent, peppery flavor.

Oak-leaf lettuce
Loose, deeply cut, divided leaves that look similar to oak leaves; crisp yet tender texture with a delicate flavor. Red oak-leaf lettuce also is available.

Spinach
Crinkled or smooth-textured leaves with long stems; somewhat earthy flavor.

Sorrel
Smooth, arrow-shaped leaves; crisp, yet tender texture with a sharp, lemonlike tang.

Mesclun

Radicchio

Arugula

Oak-leaf lettuce

Spinach

Sorrel

Swiss chard
Long flat, celerylike stalks with large, coarse leaves at the top. Red Swiss chard, also known as rhubarb chard, has ruby-colored stalks. The stems of both types have a delicate, celerylike taste, and the leaves have a hearty spinach flavor.

Kale
Frilly leaves; tough texture with a cabbagelike flavor.

Leaf lettuce
Sprawling, curly, crisp, yet tender leaves; sweet and delicate flavor. Red-tip leaf lettuce also is available.

Iceberg lettuce
Compact, smooth, round head with crisp leaves that vary from pale green in the center to medium green on the outside; mild, watery flavor.

Swiss chard

Kale

Leaf lettuce

Iceberg lettuce

Romaine
Large, elongated, sturdy leaves that branch from a white base; slightly sharp flavor. Red-tip romaine also is available.

Chinese cabbage (Napa)
Elongated, tightly packed, ruffly leaves with wide stalks; mild, sweet flavor.

Red cabbage
Round with very tightly packed reddish purple leaves; tastes similar to green cabbage.

Green cabbage
Round with very tightly packed pale green leaves; crisp and mild flavored.

Romaine

Chinese cabbage

Red cabbage

Green cabbage

Fabulous Full-Meal Salads

This chapter features an incredible array of the freshest, most flavorful main-dish salads you can imagine. From old favorites, such as Taco Salad, to exciting newcomers, such as Sesame Chicken Kabob Salad, these recipes are sure to become favorites with family and friends.

Italian Beef Salad
(See recipe, page 12.)

Italian Beef Salad

Per serving:
318 cal. (61% from fat), 20 g pro., 12 g carbo., 22 g fat,
39 mg cholesterol, 4 g dietary fiber, 516 mg sodium.

Preparation time:
10 minutes

Chilling time:
2 hours

Assembling time:
15 minutes

On special occasions use Greek kalamatra olives in this colorful, fresh-tasting salad. These purplish black olives often are cured in a wine-vinegar marinade that gives them a deliciously tangy and salty flavor.

⅓ cup red wine vinegar

¼ cup salad oil

1½ teaspoons dried minced onion

1 teaspoon dried Italian seasoning, crushed

¼ teaspoon garlic salt

⅛ teaspoon crushed red pepper

8 ounces thinly sliced cooked beef roast

6 cups torn mixed greens

1 6-ounce jar marinated artichoke hearts

1 small yellow sweet pepper, cut into strips

½ cup pitted ripe olives, drained

4 plum-shaped tomatoes, sliced

½ cup sliced fresh mushrooms

- For marinade, add the vinegar, oil, onion, Italian seasoning, garlic salt, and crushed red pepper to the Tupperware® Quick Shake® container. Apply seal and cap; shake well. Place beef in a shallow dish. Pour marinade over beef. Cover and chill for 2 to 4 hours.

- Drain beef, reserving the marinade. Arrange greens on serving platter. Drain artichoke hearts and cut any large ones in half. Arrange beef, artichoke hearts, pepper strips, olives, tomatoes, and mushrooms on greens. Drizzle with marinade. Makes 4 servings.

Note: Pictured on pages 10–11.

Beef and Apple Salad

Per serving:
330 cal. (46% from fat), 18 g pro., 27 g carbo., 17 g fat,
39 mg cholesterol, 4 g dietary fiber, 56 mg sodium.

Preparation time:
20 minutes

Dress up last night's roast beef with apples, carrots, and jicama. Then accent the combination with a sweet yet tangy apple vinaigrette dressing.

¼ cup apple juice

¼ cup salad oil

2 tablespoons red wine vinegar

Lettuce leaves

8 ounces cooked beef roast

2 medium carrots

2 medium apples, cored

1 cup jicama strips (about 4 ounces)

¼ cup raisins

- For dressing, add apple juice, salad oil, and red wine vinegar to the Tupperware Quick Shake® container. Apply seal and cap; shake well.

- Line 4 dinner plates with lettuce leaves. Cut beef into thin strips. Cut carrots into julienne strips. Cut apples into thin wedges. Arrange beef, carrots, apple wedges, and jicama strips on the lettuce-lined plates. Sprinkle each serving with raisins. Shake dressing well; pour over each serving. Makes 4 servings.

Marinated Steak Salad

Per serving:
323 cal. (66% from fat), 16 g pro., 12 g carbo., 24 g fat,
38 mg cholesterol, 2 g dietary fiber, 391 mg sodium.

**Preparation time:
35 minutes**

**Marinating time:
6 hours**

**Assembling time:
25 minutes**

Shiitake mushrooms add a rich, delicate flavor to the bed of greens. Substitute canned straw mushrooms when shiitake mushrooms are unavailable.

12	ounces boneless beef sirloin steak
½	cup olive oil or salad oil
½	cup wine vinegar
2	tablespoons dry sherry
2	tablespoons soy sauce
1	tablespoon brown sugar
1	clove garlic, minced
⅛	teaspoon ground ginger
12	cups torn mixed greens
1½	cups sliced fresh shiitake mushrooms
½	cup sliced green onions
1	tablespoon olive oil or salad oil
1	large red or green sweet pepper, cut into thin strips

- Trim fat from beef sirloin steak. Partially freeze the beef. Thinly slice across the grain into bite-size strips. Place the beef in a shallow dish or the Tupperware® Season-Serve® container.

- For marinade, add the ½ cup olive oil or salad oil, the wine vinegar, sherry, soy sauce, brown sugar, garlic, and ginger to the Tupperware Quick Shake® container. Apply seal and cap; shake well. Pour the marinade over meat. Cover dish or seal Season-Serve container. Chill in the refrigerator for 6 to 24 hours, turning meat in dish or inverting Season-Serve container occasionally to distribute marinade.

- To serve, toss together greens, shiitake mushrooms, and green onions in a large bowl. Divide the mixture among 6 dinner plates; set aside.

- Drain meat, reserving ⅔ *cup* marinade. Pour the 1 tablespoon oil into a large skillet. (Add more oil as necessary during cooking.) Preheat over medium-high heat. Add pepper strips; stir-fry for 2 minutes or until crisp-tender. Remove pepper strips from the skillet.

- Add meat to the skillet; stir-fry for 2 to 3 minutes or to desired doneness. Return pepper strips to the skillet; push meat and pepper strips from the center of skillet. Add reserved marinade to the center of the skillet. Cook and stir until bubbly. Stir all the ingredients in the skillet together. Divide the hot meat mixture among the dinner plates. Serve immediately. Makes 6 servings.

Ready-Cooked Beef

If a recipe calls for cooked beef, you can save time by purchasing it at the deli counter in your supermarket. Or, cook your own meat. A three-pound roast will give you about seven cups of cooked meat.

For roasting, choose a tender cut, such as round tip roast. Place the meat, fat side up, on a rack in a shallow roasting pan. Do not add water or liquid and do not cover. Roast in a 325° oven for about 1¾ hours or until a meat thermometer registers 160° for medium doneness.

If cooking a pot roast, choose a boneless chuck roast. Trim fat from roast. In a Dutch oven, brown roast on all sides in hot oil. Drain fat. Pour ¾ cup liquid over pot roast. (Water or beef broth are good choices.) Bring to boiling; reduce heat. Cover and simmer 1¾ to 2 hours or until meat is tender.

Taco Salad

Per serving:
422 cal. (50% from fat), 32 g pro., 21 g carbo., 24 g fat,
100 mg cholesterol, 7 g dietary fiber, 789 mg sodium.

**Preparation time:
25 minutes**

Another time, serve this spicy meat mixture over homemade tortilla chips. To make tortilla chips, cut corn or flour tortillas into wedges. Place the wedges on a baking sheet and bake in a 350° oven about 10 minutes or until crisp.

1	pound ground beef or ground raw turkey
3	cloves garlic, minced
1	16-ounce can dark red kidney beans
1	8-ounce jar taco sauce
1	tablespoon chili powder
2	cups chopped tomatoes
2	cups shredded cheddar cheese (8 ounces)
1	cup chopped green pepper
½	cup sliced pitted ripe olives
¼	cup sliced green onions
	Salad savoy leaves
	Corn Sticks (see recipe below) (optional)

- Cook beef or turkey and garlic in a large skillet until meat is no longer pink. Drain off fat. Stir in *undrained* kidney beans, taco sauce, and chili powder. Bring to boiling; reduce heat. Cover and simmer for 10 minutes.

- Meanwhile, combine tomatoes, cheese, green pepper, olives, and green onions in a large bowl; add hot meat mixture. Toss lightly to mix. Line 6 dinner plates with salad savoy leaves. Divide salad mixture among plates. Serve with Corn Sticks, if desired. Makes 6 servings.

Note: If you like, serve this salad with avocado slices, sprigs of cilantro, lime wedges, sour cream, sliced ripe olives, and chopped tomato.

Quick Corn Sticks

The next time taco salad is on the menu, round out the meal with a Southwestern-style accompaniment—corn sticks or corn muffins. Their wonderful corn flavor and light texture are a perfect match for the salad's zesty meat topping.

Corn Sticks or Muffins: Stir together 1 cup all-purpose *flour*, 1 cup *yellow cornmeal*, 2 to 4 tablespoons *sugar*, 1 tablespoon *baking powder*, and ½ teaspoon *salt* in a mixing bowl. Beat together 2 *eggs*, 1 cup *milk*, and ¼ cup *cooking oil* in another bowl. Add to flour mixture and stir just until the batter is smooth (*do not overbeat*). Spoon batter into greased corn stick pans or muffin pans, filling pans ⅔ full. Bake in a 425° oven for 12 to 15 minutes or until golden brown. Makes 8 or 9 corn sticks or muffins.

Note: Use the 4 tablespoons sugar if you prefer sweeter corn sticks or muffins.

Per corn stick: 227 cal. (36% from fat), 6 g pro., 30 g carbo., 9 g fat, 56 mg cholesterol, 1 g dietary fiber, 284 mg sodium.

Taco Salad

Beef and Pasta Salad with Garlic Dressing

Per serving:
453 cal. (52% from fat), 23 g pro., 31 g carbo., 26 g fat,
58 mg cholesterol, 2 g dietary fiber, 230 mg sodium.

**Preparation time:
30 minutes**

**Chilling time:
4 hours**

Using Italian herb seasoning is a convenient way to flavor this creamy pasta salad. To make your own seasoning blend, combine equal amounts of oregano, basil, ground red pepper, rosemary, and, if desired, garlic powder.

1	cup packaged dried corkscrew macaroni
1	cup fresh green beans cut into 2-inch lengths
8	ounces cooked beef roast, cut into thin strips (1½ cups)
1	medium red onion, chopped
1	medium carrot, shredded
½	cup sliced radishes
½	cup mayonnaise
½	cup plain yogurt
2	teaspoons white wine vinegar or vinegar
2	cloves garlic, minced
½	teaspoon dried Italian herb seasoning, crushed
¼	teaspoon dry mustard
1	to 2 tablespoons milk

- Cook pasta according to package directions. Drain pasta. Rinse with cold water; drain again.

- Meanwhile, cook the green beans in a small amount of boiling salted water for 20 to 25 minutes or until crisp-tender. Drain beans. Rinse with cold water; drain again.

- Combine the cooked pasta, green beans, beef, the onion, carrot, and radishes in a large bowl.

- For dressing, stir together mayonnaise, yogurt, vinegar, garlic, Italian herb seasoning, dry mustard, and ¼ teaspoon *salt*. Pour dressing over pasta mixture. Toss to coat. Cover and chill for 4 to 24 hours.

- If necessary, stir milk into the pasta mixture before serving. Makes 4 servings.

Beef Salad with Fresh Basil Dressing

Per serving:
243 cal. (44% from fat), 20 g pro., 14 g carbo., 12 g fat,
46 mg cholesterol, 3 g dietary fiber, 267 mg sodium.

**Preparation time:
30 minutes**

Parsnips add unexpected flavor and freshness to this salad. Look for small, evenly shaped parsnips—they're more tender.

8	ounces lean cooked beef roast
6	cups torn mixed greens
½	cup thinly sliced parsnips
½	cup thinly sliced carrot
½	cup sliced zucchini
½	cup broccoli flowerets
	Fresh Basil Dressing (see recipe at right)
½	of a 16-ounce can julienne beets, well drained

- Cut beef roast into thin strips. Combine greens, beef roast, parsnips, carrot, zucchini, and broccoli flowerets in a large bowl. Toss lightly to mix. Pour Fresh Basil Dressing over salad. Toss lightly to coat. Top with drained beets. Makes 4 servings.

Fresh Basil Dressing: Stir together: ½ cup *buttermilk;* 3 tablespoons *mayonnaise;* 1 tablespoon snipped *fresh basil* or 1 teaspoon *dried basil,* crushed; 1 tablespoon *lemon juice;* 1 teaspoon *sugar;* and dash *pepper.* Cover and store in the refrigerator for up to 2 weeks.

Oriental Broiled Beef Salad

Per serving:
477 cal. (71% from fat), 23 g pro., 12 g carbo., 38 g fat, 57 mg cholesterol, 3 g dietary fiber, 68 mg sodium.

Preparation time: 8 minutes

Marinating time: 6 hours

Assembling time: 15 minutes

Enjoy the tantalizing flavor of sizzling steak served over crisp greens and colorful vegetables. Just for fun, serve this salad with chopsticks.

½ cup salad oil

½ cup rice wine vinegar or white wine vinegar

2 teaspoons toasted sesame oil

1 teaspoon sugar

1 teaspoon grated gingerroot

¼ teaspoon ground red pepper

2 cloves garlic, minced

12 ounces boneless beef sirloin steak, cut 1 inch thick

3 cups torn romaine

3 cups torn curly endive

1 large red or yellow sweet pepper, cut into strips

1 cup baby pear tomatoes or cherry tomatoes, halved

1 cup enoki mushrooms

¼ cup chopped pistachio nuts

- For dressing, add salad oil, vinegar, sesame oil, sugar, gingerroot, red pepper, and garlic to the Tupperware® Quick Shake® container. Apply seal and cap; shake well.

- Place steak in a shallow dish. Pour ⅓ cup dressing into dish. Cover dish. Chill in the refrigerator for 6 to 24 hours, turning meat in dish occasionally to distribute marinade. Cover and refrigerate the remaining dressing.

- Remove steak from dish, reserving marinade. Place steak on unheated rack of broiler pan. Broil 4 to 5 inches from heat for 6 minutes. Turn and brush with reserved marinade. Broil to desired doneness allowing 6 to 9 minutes more for medium.

- For salad, in a very large bowl combine romaine, curly endive, sweet pepper strips, tomatoes, and enoki mushrooms. Toss lightly to mix. Divide salad mixture among 4 dinner plates. Thinly slice broiled steak and divide into 4 equal portions. Top each salad with meat. Sprinkle with pistachio nuts. Drizzle the reserved dressing over salads. Makes 4 servings.

Grilling directions: Place steak on rack of an uncovered grill directly over *medium-hot* coals. Grill for 6 minutes. Turn; brush with reserved marinade. Grill to desired doneness; allow 6 to 9 minutes for medium.

A Medley of Mushrooms

Brown or white, mild or nutty—mushrooms come in many varieties, adding interest and flavor to salads. Common or button mushrooms are the kind sold most often. They can be white, cream colored, or brown and have a mild flavor and the familiar umbrella shape. Chanterelle are mild mushrooms shaped like golden trumpets. Enoki mushrooms, an Oriental variety, are mild-flavored with long slender stems and tiny caps. Shiitake mushrooms are rich-tasting, large brown Oriental mushrooms with floppy caps. And straw mushrooms, another Oriental variety, have an umbrella shape and a mild flavor.

When selecting mushrooms, look for firm, fresh ones that are plump and have no bruises, spots, or moistness. Avoid any that are slimy. Store the mushrooms, unwashed, in the refrigerator for a day or two. Leave prepackaged mushrooms in their package. Store loose mushrooms in a paper—not plastic—bag.

*Marinated Ham and
Tortellini Salad*

Marinated Ham and Tortellini Salad

Per serving:
584 cal. (51% from fat), 28 g pro., 45 g carbo., 34 g fat,
71 mg cholesterol, 3 g dietary fiber, 1,166 mg sodium.

Preparation time:
20 minutes

Chilling time:
4 hours

Assembling time:
10 minutes

Tortellini (little pasta rings with a stuffing inside) also comes dried. You can use 6 ounces of the dried to replace the 9 ounces of refrigerated pasta.

1	9-ounce package refrigerated cheese-filled spinach or regular tortellini
½	cup salad oil
¼	cup lemon juice
¼	cup orange juice
1	tablespoon Dijon-style mustard
1	teaspoon dried basil, crushed
1	clove garlic, minced
¼	teaspoon pepper
8	ounces fully cooked ham, cut into bite-size pieces
1	cup cauliflower flowerets
4	cups assorted greens
2	medium orange or red sweet peppers, cut into rings

- Cook pasta according to package directions. Drain pasta. Rinse with cold water. Drain again.

- For marinade, add salad oil, lemon juice, orange juice, mustard, basil, garlic, and pepper to the Tupperware® Quick Shake® container. Apply seal and cap; shake well.

- Place pasta in a shallow dish or the Tupperware Season-Serve® container. Shake marinade mixture again and pour over pasta. Add ham and cauliflower and toss well. Cover dish or seal container. Chill for 4 to 24 hours, stirring mixture in dish or inverting Season-Serve container several times to distribute marinade.

- To serve, line 4 dinner plates with assorted greens. Place pepper rings on greens. Spoon pasta mixture over top. Makes 4 servings.

Ham and Vegetable Toss

Per serving:
183 cal. (38% from fat), 19 g pro., 11 g carbo., 8 g fat,
40 mg cholesterol, 4 g dietary fiber, 897 mg sodium.

Preparation time:
30 minutes

Make this savory salad ahead of time, if you like. Simply leave out the greens until just before serving.

4	cups torn mixed greens
1	cup shredded red cabbage
8	ounces lean fully cooked ham, cut into bite-size strips
1	cup sliced cauliflower flowerets
1	cup frozen peas, thawed
¼	cup sliced radishes
½	cup Dijon Dressing (see recipe at right)

- Combine mixed greens and red cabbage in a large bowl. Add ham, cauliflower, peas, and radishes. Toss lightly to mix. Pour Dijon Dressing over salad. Toss lightly to coat. Makes 4 servings.

Dijon Dressing: In a small bowl, stir together one 8-ounce carton *dairy sour cream*, ½ cup *milk*, 2 tablespoons *Dijon-style mustard*, 1 tablespoon snipped *parsley*, and 2 teaspoons snipped *fresh dill* or ½ teaspoon *dried dillweed*. Cover and store in the refrigerator for up to 1 week. Makes about 1½ cups (twelve 2-tablespoon servings).

Minted Ham Salad

Per serving:
293 cal. (44% from fat), 29 g pro., 12 g carbo., 14 g fat,
62 mg cholesterol, 3 g dietary fiber, 1,629 mg sodium.

Preparation time:
20 minutes

Chilling time:
4 hours

Serve this elegant yogurt-dressed salad with crisp crackers or bread sticks.

1   8-ounce carton plain yogurt

1   tablespoon milk

2   teaspoons horseradish mustard

1   tablespoon fresh snipped mint or 1 teaspoon dried mint, crushed

⅛   teaspoon onion powder

1½   cups broccoli flowerets

1   cup sliced carrot

½   cup jicama pieces (about 2 ounces)

1   pound extra-lean fully cooked boneless ham

½   cup shredded cheddar cheese (2 ounces)

- Combine yogurt, milk, mustard, mint, and onion powder in a bowl. Add broccoli, carrot, and jicama. Toss to coat.

- Cut ham into ½-inch cubes. Add ham and shredded cheddar cheese to vegetable mixture; toss to mix. Chill for 4 to 24 hours. If desired, garnish salad with fresh mint leaves. Makes 4 servings.

Ham and Fruit Salad

Per serving:
530 cal. (57% from fat), 30 g pro., 28 g carbo., 34 g fat,
82 mg cholesterol, 3 g dietary fiber, 1,060 mg sodium.

Preparation time:
25 minutes

Serve this sweet and spicy salad with freshly baked muffins and a citrus punch for a spectacular brunch.

8   ounces thinly sliced lean fully cooked ham

8   ounces thinly sliced Monterey Jack or Muenster cheese

    Lettuce leaves

2   cups sliced, peeled peaches or frozen peach slices, thawed

2   kiwi fruit, peeled and sliced

1   cup seedless grapes, halved

    Honey-Mustard Vinaigrette (see recipe at right)

- Roll up each slice of ham; secure with a wooden pick. Repeat with cheese slices.

- Line 4 dinner plates with lettuce leaves. Arrange ham and cheese rolls, peach slices, kiwi fruit, and grapes on the lettuce-lined plates.

- Pour Honey-Mustard Vinaigrette over each serving. Makes 4 servings.

Honey-Mustard Vinaigrette: Add ¼ cup *salad oil*, ¼ cup *vinegar*, 1 tablespoon *honey*, ¼ teaspoon *dry mustard*, and ⅛ teaspoon *pepper* to the Tupperware® Quick Shake® container. Apply seal and cap; shake well.

Mix-and-Match Chef's Salad

Per serving:
355 cal. (69% from fat), 21 g pro., 7 g carbo., 27 g fat,
65 mg cholesterol, 2 g dietary fiber, 792 mg sodium.

**Preparation time:
20 minutes**

This hearty salad is so versatile. Just mix and match meats, cheeses, and vegetables for a different salad every time!

⅓ cup mayonnaise

3 tablespoons dairy sour cream

1 tablespoon snipped parsley

1 tablespoon snipped chives

1 tablespoon tarragon vinegar

2 teaspoons anchovy paste

6 cups torn salad greens

6 ounces fully cooked ham or beef roast

4 ounces Swiss or cheddar cheese, cut into ¼-inch cubes

1 cup sliced fresh mushrooms or halved cherry tomatoes

¾ cup sliced radishes or cucumber

½ cup shredded carrot or chopped green pepper

- For dressing, combine mayonnaise, sour cream, parsley, chives, tarragon vinegar, and anchovy paste in a blender container or food processor bowl. Cover and blend or process until smooth. If desired, cover and chill.

- Combine torn greens, ham or beef roast, cheese, mushrooms, radishes, and carrot in a large bowl. Pour dressing over salad. Toss to coat. Makes 4 servings.

Dressing Your Salads

Diners watching their intake of calories or fat should keep an eye on what their salads are wearing. How your salads are dressed often determines whether they're a dieter's loyal friend—or an undermining foe. Here are three tips to make sure your salads are dressed right.

Learn to read—bottle labels, that is. Reduced-calorie dressings can have up to three-fourths fewer calories than their classic counterparts.

Play one-on-one. For oil and vinegar salad dressings, use equal parts oil and vinegar rather than the typical 3-to-1 ratio. A mild vinegar such as balsamic will help reduce the tartness of the extra vinegar in the dressing.

Stir in a substitute. Cut the fat and calories in creamy dressings by stirring in some plain low-fat yogurt. Your taste buds won't know the difference—but your waistline will.

Chicken Salad with Blue Cheese Dressing

Per serving:
199 cal. (34% from fat), 21 g pro., 12 g carbo., 8 g fat,
55 mg cholesterol, 3 g dietary fiber, 186 mg sodium.

Preparation time:
20 minutes

Sage stems and nasturtiums make an easy and elegant garnish for this refreshing luncheon salad.

1½ cups chopped cooked chicken or turkey

2 medium tomatoes, cut into wedges

1 cup jicama strips (about 4 ounces)

1 medium yellow or green sweet pepper, cut into 1-inch squares

8 cups mesclun or torn assorted greens

½ cup Blue Cheese Dressing (see recipe at right)

- Combine chicken or turkey, tomato, jicama, and sweet pepper in a large bowl. Line 4 dinner plates with mesclun. Spoon chicken mixture on top of greens. Pour Blue Cheese Dressing over salad on each plate. If desired, sprinkle additional crumbled blue cheese on salads. Makes 4 servings.

Blue Cheese Dressing: In a blender container or food processor bowl, combine: ½ cup *dairy sour cream;* ¼ cup *cream-style cottage cheese;* ¼ cup crumbled *blue cheese;* 1 *green onion,* thinly sliced; ½ teaspoon finely shredded *lemon peel;* 1 teaspoon *lemon juice;* and ⅛ teaspoon *salt.* Cover and blend or process until smooth. Stir in enough *milk* (1 to 2 tablespoons) to make of desired consistency. Cover and store in the refrigerator for up to 2 weeks. Makes about 1 cup (eight 2-tablespoon servings).

Southwestern Chicken Salad

Per serving:
284 cal. (32% from fat), 31 g pro., 19 g carbo., 10 g fat,
72 mg cholesterol, 6 g dietary fiber, 396 mg sodium.

Preparation time:
10 minutes

Chilling time:
4 hours

Cooking time:
25 minutes

The lively combination of chili peppers, cilantro, garlic, and tomatoes in the salsa dressing enhances the flavor of grilled chicken and vegetables arranged on a bed of greens.

8 yellow sunburst squash or pattypan squash

4 small zucchini, halved lengthwise

2 large red, yellow, and/or green sweet peppers, cut into 1-inch-wide strips

2 tablespoons margarine or butter, melted

4 large skinless, boneless chicken breast halves (about 1 pound total)

Salad savoy or curly endive leaves

Chunky Salsa (see recipe at right)

- Precook squash, covered, in a small amount of boiling water for 3 minutes. Drain. Halve squash. Generously brush squash, zucchini, and sweet peppers with melted margarine. Rinse chicken; pat dry. Grill chicken on an uncovered grill directly over *medium-hot* coals for 15 to 18 minutes or until tender and no longer pink; turn once. Cook vegetables on grill with chicken until tender and slightly charred, turning often. Allow about 18 minutes for squash, 8 to 10 minutes for peppers, and 5 to 6 minutes for zucchini. (Lay vegetables on rack perpendicular to bars so they don't drop through.)

- Line 4 dinner plates with savoy or endive leaves. Diagonally cut breast halves into slices; reassemble breast halves on top of greens. Divide vegetables among plates. Pour *half* of the Chunky Salsa over salads. Pass the remaining Chunky Salsa. Makes 4 servings.

Chunky Salsa: Stir together: 1½ cups finely chopped, peeled *tomatoes;* ½ of a 4-ounce can diced *green chili peppers,* drained; ¼ cup sliced *green onions;* 2 tablespoons chopped *green pepper;* 2 tablespoons snipped *fresh cilantro;* 2 tablespoons *lemon juice;* 1 clove *garlic,* minced; and ⅛ teaspoon *ground black pepper.* Place about *1 cup* of the tomato mixture and ¼ cup *tomato sauce* in a blender container. Cover and blend just until smooth. Stir into remaining tomato mixture. Cover and chill 4 to 24 hours, stirring occasionally.

Chicken Salad with Blue
Cheese Dressing

Turkey-Strawberry Salad

Per serving:
207 cal. (33% from fat), 22 g pro., 14 g carbo., 8 g fat,
55 mg cholesterol, 3 g dietary fiber, 148 mg sodium.

Preparation time:
25 minutes

Subtly sweet aptly describes this colorful mix of strawberries, turkey, sweet pepper, and spinach.

4 cups torn spinach

1 pint fresh strawberries, halved

4 green onions, bias sliced

12 ounces turkey breast tenderloin steaks

2 tablespoons olive oil or salad oil

1 tablespoon red wine vinegar

1 tablespoon water

½ teaspoon dried minced onion

⅛ teaspoon salt

½ of a yellow sweet pepper, sliced into rings

1 tablespoon honey

- Toss together torn spinach, halved strawberries, and bias-sliced green onions in a large bowl; set aside. Rinse turkey breast tenderloin steaks; pat dry. Cut turkey into bite-size strips; set aside.

- For dressing, combine oil, vinegar, water, dried onion, and salt. Heat *half* of the dressing in a large skillet. Add the pepper rings. Stir-fry for 1½ to 2 minutes or until crisp-tender. Remove pepper rings from the skillet.

- Heat the remaining dressing in the same skillet. Stir-fry the turkey strips in the hot dressing for 2 to 3 minutes or until no longer pink. Remove from heat. Stir in pepper rings and honey. Pour turkey mixture over spinach mixture. Toss well. Makes 4 servings.

Note: Pictured on the cover.

Curried Pasta and Chicken Salad

Per serving:
370 cal. (53% from fat), 23 g pro., 22 g carbo., 22 g fat,
61 mg cholesterol, 2 g dietary fiber, 296 mg sodium.

Preparation time:
25 minutes

Chilling time:
4 hours

Give this fruited chicken salad a different look by using another shape of pasta in place of the elbow macaroni. Try shells, spirals, wagon wheels, tiny tubes, or alphabet letters.

2 ounces elbow macaroni

1½ cups chopped cooked chicken (about 8 ounces)

1 cup coarsely chopped apple

⅓ cup chopped celery

¼ cup finely chopped onion

⅓ cup mayonnaise

⅓ cup plain yogurt

½ teaspoon curry powder

⅛ teaspoon salt

¼ cup cashews or peanuts

1 to 2 tablespoons milk

Lettuce leaves

- Cook pasta according to package directions. Drain pasta. Rinse with cold water. Drain again.

- Combine cooked pasta, chicken, apple, celery, and onion in a large bowl.

- For dressing, mix mayonnaise, yogurt, curry powder, and salt in a small bowl. Pour dressing over pasta mixture. Toss to coat. Cover and chill for 4 to 24 hours.

- To serve, stir cashews or peanuts into pasta mixture. If necessary, stir in milk to give the salad a creamy consistency. Serve in lettuce-lined bowls. Makes 4 servings.

Spicy Chicken Salad

Per serving:
659 cal. (62% from fat), 29 g pro., 35 g carbo., 47 g fat,
168 mg cholesterol, 4 g dietary fiber, 450 mg sodium.

**Preparation time:
40 minutes**

Crisp oven-fried chicken strips sport a peppery cornmeal coating in this hearty salad. Just add crusty Italian bread to round out the meal.

2   large skinless, boneless chicken breast halves (about 8 ounces total)

¼   cup cornmeal

½   teaspoon dried thyme, crushed

¼   teaspoon onion powder

¼   teaspoon garlic salt

¼   teaspoon ground red pepper

2   tablespoons margarine or butter, melted

4   cups torn spinach

4   cups torn leaf lettuce

2   cups sliced fresh mushrooms

1   cup cubed Swiss cheese (4 ounces)

12   cherry tomatoes, halved

½   cup Honey-Mustard Dressing (see recipe, above right)

2   hard-cooked eggs, sliced

• Rinse chicken; pat dry. Cut chicken into bite-size strips. Combine cornmeal, thyme, onion powder, garlic salt, red pepper, and ¼ teaspoon *ground black pepper* in a shallow bowl. Dip chicken strips in melted margarine. Dip strips in cornmeal mixture to coat. Place chicken strips in a single layer on an ungreased baking sheet. Bake in a 400° oven 8 to 10 minutes or until chicken is tender and no longer pink, turning once.

• Meanwhile, combine spinach, leaf lettuce, mushrooms, cheese, and cherry tomatoes in a large bowl. Add the hot chicken strips. Pour Honey-Mustard Dressing over salad. Toss lightly to coat. Arrange egg slices around edge of bowl. Makes 4 servings.

Honey-Mustard Dressing: Combine ¼ cup *honey*, 3 tablespoons *white wine vinegar* or *white vinegar*, 2 tablespoons *coarse-grain brown mustard*, and 1 clove *garlic*, minced, in a small bowl or blender container. Beating with an electric mixer on medium speed or with blender running slowly, add ½ cup *salad oil* in a thin, steady stream. Continue beating or blending mixture about 3 minutes or until dressing is thick. Makes about 1 cup (eight 2-tablespoon servings).

Fresh and Fabulous Spinach

The hearty flavor and crisp texture of spinach add extra zing to salads. To ensure the spinach you use is in tip-top shape:

Buy spinach with dark leaves that are free of moisture and mold. Skip bunches that have wilted or bruised leaves.

Wash spinach by placing the leaves in a large bowl of cold water. After a few minutes, remove the greens and replace the water. Then dunk the greens several times in the fresh water until no more dirt or sand collects in the bowl. If you're pressed for time, purchase packages of prewashed spinach leaves.

Store spinach by patting the leaves dry and placing them in a Tupperware® brand container lined with a paper towel. (If you're using prewashed spinach, leave it in the store packaging.) Refrigerate the spinach for up to 3 days.

Cobb Salad

Cobb Salad

Per serving:
483 cal. (68% from fat), 32 g pro., 8 g carbo., 36 g fat,
182 mg cholesterol, 2 g dietary fiber, 587 mg sodium.

**Preparation time:
25 minutes**

This artfully arranged chicken and avocado salad was first created at the Brown Derby Restaurant in Los Angeles. Now it has become an American classic, appearing on menus and dinner tables throughout the country.

6 cups shredded lettuce

3 cups chopped cooked chicken (1 pound)

3 hard-cooked eggs, chopped

2 medium tomatoes, seeded and chopped

¾ cup crumbled blue cheese (3 ounces)

6 slices bacon, crisp-cooked, drained, and crumbled

1 medium avocado, seeded, peeled, and cut into wedges

Small Belgian endive leaves

Brown Derby French Dressing (see recipe, above right)

- Place shredded lettuce on 6 dinner plates. Evenly divide chicken, hard-cooked eggs, tomatoes, blue cheese, and crumbled bacon among plates, arranging each in a row on top of the lettuce. Place avocado wedges and endive leaves to the side. If desired, garnish with calendula blossoms. Serve with Brown Derby French Dressing. Makes 6 servings.

Brown Derby French Dressing: Add ⅓ cup *red wine vinegar*, 1 tablespoon *lemon juice*, 1 teaspoon *Worcestershire sauce*, ½ teaspoon *salt*, ½ teaspoon *sugar*, ½ teaspoon *dry mustard*, ½ teaspoon *pepper*, and 1 clove *garlic*, minced, to the Tupperware® Quick Shake® container. Apply seal and cap; shake well. Add ½ cup *olive oil* or *salad oil;* seal and shake vigorously. If desired, chill thoroughly. Shake before serving.

Lemon Chicken Salad

Per serving:
408 cal. (65% from fat), 24 g pro., 12 g carbo., 30 g fat,
76 mg cholesterol, 2 g dietary fiber, 231 mg sodium.

**Preparation time:
20 minutes**

**Chilling time:
1 hour**

Perk up your lunch menu with this cool, refreshing salad. For a chicken salad sandwich, spoon the salad mixture into four large pita bread rounds, split and lined with lettuce leaves.

2 cups chopped cooked chicken or turkey (about 10 ounces)

½ cup sliced celery

⅓ cup shredded carrot

2 tablespoons thinly sliced green onion

½ cup mayonnaise

1 teaspoon finely shredded lemon peel

1 tablespoon lemon juice

1 cup seedless grapes, halved, or one 8-ounce can pineapple tidbits, drained

Lettuce leaves

¼ cup slivered or sliced almonds, toasted

- Combine chicken or turkey, celery, carrot, and green onion in a large bowl.

- For dressing, stir together mayonnaise, lemon peel, and lemon juice in a small bowl. Stir into the chicken mixture. Cover and chill for 1 to 24 hours.

- To serve, stir in the grapes or pineapple. Divide chicken mixture among 4 lettuce-lined dinner plates. Sprinkle with almonds. Makes 4 servings.

Next-Day Chicken Fiesta Salad

Per serving:
418 cal. (55% from fat), 27 g pro., 22 g carbo., 26 g fat,
69 mg cholesterol, 7 g dietary fiber, 607 mg sodium.

Preparation time:
30 minutes

Chilling time:
4 hours

A spicy avocado dressing provides the finishing touch for this seven-layer salad which can be made ahead for a busy day.

4   cups torn iceberg or Bibb lettuce

2   small tomatoes

½   cup shredded Monterey Jack cheese with jalapeño peppers

1   8-ounce can red kidney beans, rinsed and drained

1½   cups chopped cooked chicken or turkey

1   cup jicama strips (about 4 ounces)

½   cup sliced pitted ripe olives (optional)

    Avocado Dressing (see recipe, above right)

¾   cup slightly crushed tortilla chips

- Place lettuce in the bottom of a large bowl. Cut tomatoes into thin wedges. Layer in the following order: cheese, beans, chicken or turkey, tomatoes, jicama, and, if desired, olives. Spread Avocado Dressing over the top of the salad, sealing to the edge of the bowl. Cover and chill for 4 to 24 hours.

- To serve, sprinkle with the crushed tortilla chips. Makes 4 servings.

  Avocado Dressing: In blender container or food processor bowl combine: 1 small *avocado*, seeded, peeled, and cut up; ¼ cup *mayonnaise*; 2 tablespoons *chopped canned green chili peppers*; 2 tablespoons *lemon juice*; ½ teaspoon *chili powder*; ¼ teaspoon *salt*; and 1 clove *garlic*, minced. Cover and blend or process until the dressing is smooth.

Hot German Bean Salad

Per serving:
222 cal. (11% from fat), 22 g pro., 34 g carbo., 3 g fat,
30 mg cholesterol, 4 g dietary fiber, 736 mg sodium.

Preparation time:
20 minutes

This off-the-shelf dinner is a nutritious take-off of German potato salad. Fiber-rich beans and lean chicken take the place of potatoes and bacon.

1   medium carrot

½   of a small red onion

    Nonstick spray coating

1   stalk celery, sliced

¼   cup vinegar

1   tablespoon sugar

1   tablespoon cornstarch

1   teaspoon instant beef bouillon granules

¼   teaspoon celery seed

1   15-ounce can black beans, rinsed and drained

1   8-ounce can red kidney beans, rinsed and drained

1   cup chopped cooked chicken

- Chop carrot and onion. Spray a cold large skillet with nonstick coating. Heat skillet over medium heat. Stir-fry chopped carrot, chopped onion, and sliced celery in the hot skillet for 2 minutes. Remove from heat.

- Stir together ½ cup *water*, the vinegar, sugar, cornstarch, beef bouillon granules, and celery seed in a small bowl. Add to skillet. Cook and stir over medium-high heat for 1 to 2 minutes or until mixture is thickened and bubbly.

- Stir in black beans, kidney beans, and cooked chicken. Cook for 2 to 3 minutes more or until heated through, stirring occasionally. Makes 4 servings.

Oriental Chicken Pasta Salad

Per serving:
481 cal. (34% from fat), 27 g pro., 51 g carbo., 18 g fat,
48 mg cholesterol, 2 g dietary fiber, 830 mg sodium.

**Preparation time:
25 minutes**

**Chilling time:
2 hours**

Toasted sesame oil adds a wonderfully nutty flavor to this salad. Look for it in an Oriental food store or the specialty food section of a supermarket. (When shopping for toasted sesame oil, don't confuse it with its untoasted cousin, labeled simply sesame oil.)

8 ounces spaghetti, broken

½ of an 8-ounce package frozen baby corn

1 small cucumber

1 small red or green sweet pepper

1½ cups chopped cooked chicken (8 ounces)

1 medium carrot, thinly bias-sliced

2 green onions, thinly sliced

⅓ cup tarragon vinegar

¼ cup salad oil

3 tablespoons soy sauce

1 teaspoon toasted sesame oil

½ teaspoon sugar

½ teaspoon dry mustard

Dash bottled hot pepper sauce

- Cook pasta according to package directions. Drain pasta. Rinse with cold water. Drain again.

- Cook corn according to package directions. Drain corn. Rinse with cold water. Drain again. Thinly bias-slice cucumber. Cut pepper into bite-size strips.

- Combine the cooked pasta, corn, cucumber, red or green sweet pepper, chicken, carrot, and green onions in a large bowl. Toss gently to mix.

- For dressing, add the vinegar, salad oil, soy sauce, toasted sesame oil, sugar, dry mustard, and bottled hot pepper sauce to the Tupperware® Quick Shake® container. Apply seal and cap; shake well. Pour dressing over the pasta mixture. Toss to coat. Cover and chill for 2 to 24 hours.

- To serve, gently toss pasta mixture. Serve on 4 dinner plates. Makes 4 servings.

Pasta Primer

Choosing just the right shape of pasta can make the difference between a unique pasta salad and a boring one. Some types of pasta work best in salads because they hold the dressing well. These include large bow ties, cavatelli, ditalini (thimbles), elbow macaroni, mostaccioli, rigatoni, rotini (corkscrew noodles), shells, spaetzle, tortellini, and wagon wheels. For convenience, store pasta in Tupperware® Modular Mates® containers.

To cook the pasta, place 3 quarts of water for every 4 to 8 ounces of pasta in a large pan. Bring the water to boiling. Add the pasta. Reduce heat; boil, uncovered, for the time listed below or until the pasta is tender but still firm.

Ditalini, small shells	7 to 9 minutes
Large bow ties, elbow macaroni, rotini	8 to 10 minutes
Cavatelli, spaetzle, wagon wheels	10 to 12 minutes
Mostaccioli, large shells	12 to 14 minutes
Rigatoni, tortellini	15 minutes

Sesame Chicken Kabob Salad

Per serving:
355 cal. (47% from fat), 29 g pro., 18 g carbo., 19 g fat,
72 mg cholesterol, 2 g dietary fiber, 413 mg sodium.

**Preparation time:
30 minutes**

Give the radish slices a fun shape by turning them into spinning tops. Thinly slice about five radishes. Cutting from the center to the edge, make a notch in each slice. Then, holding two slices, line up the notches and press the slices together.

4   medium skinless, boneless chicken breast halves

16   fresh pineapple chunks

3   tablespoons salad oil

3   tablespoons rice vinegar

1   tablespoon toasted sesame oil

1   tablespoon soy sauce

½   teaspoon dry mustard

1   tablespoon plum sauce

2   cups chopped red cabbage

2   cups chopped bok choy

16   to 24 fresh pea pods

½   cup enoki mushrooms

½   cup sliced radishes

Toasted sesame seed

- Rinse chicken and pat dry with paper towels. Cut each chicken breast half into 4 lengthwise strips. Soak eight 6-inch or four 12-inch wooden skewers in water for 30 minutes. Thread the chicken strips and pieces of pineapple on the skewers. Place kabobs on the unheated rack of a broiler pan.

- For dressing, add the salad oil, vinegar, toasted sesame oil, soy sauce, and dry mustard to the Tupperware® Quick Shake® container. Apply seal and cap; shake until combined. Reserve *2 tablespoons* dressing. Cover remaining dressing; chill until needed.

- Stir together the 2 tablespoons reserved dressing and plum sauce in a small bowl.

- Broil kabobs 4 to 5 inches from the heat for 5 minutes or until lightly browned. Turn kabobs; brush with sauce mixture. Broil 3 to 5 minutes more or until chicken is tender and no longer pink.

- Combine cabbage and bok choy; divide among 4 dinner plates. Trim pea pods. Top cabbage mixture with kabobs, pea pods, mushrooms, and radishes. Shake dressing to combine; drizzle over each salad. Sprinkle with sesame seed. Makes 4 servings.

Buying Salad Ingredients

Many salad recipes call for cup measures of ingredients, but when you're at the supermarket, it's often difficult to know how much of an ingredient to buy. Here's a handy chart to help you with your salad ingredient math.

Amount of Ingredient Purchased	Cup Measure
1 medium head Bibb lettuce	3 cups torn
1 pound broccoli	3½ cups flowerets
1 pound cabbage	5 cups shredded
2 medium carrots	1 cup sliced
1½ pounds cauliflower	4 cups flowerets
1 medium cucumber	1¾ cups sliced
1 large green pepper	1 cup chopped
1 small head iceberg lettuce	7½ cups torn
8 ounces mushrooms	3 cups sliced
1 medium onion	½ cup chopped
1 pound spinach	12 cups torn
1 medium tomato	1 cup chopped
1 medium zucchini	2 cups sliced

Sesame Chicken Kabob Salad

Pastrami Salad Dijon

Per serving:
290 cal. (53% from fat), 21 g pro., 15 g carbo., 18 g fat, 55 mg cholesterol, 4 g dietary fiber, 1,192 mg sodium.

**Preparation time:
20 minutes**

Look for turkey pastrami at your supermarket deli. If it's unavailable, use regular pastrami instead.

6   cups torn fresh spinach

½   of a medium cucumber, halved lengthwise and sliced

2   cups shredded red and/or green cabbage

12   ounces thinly sliced turkey pastrami

½   cup plain croutons

¼   cup mayonnaise

¼   cup plain yogurt

1   tablespoon Dijon-style mustard

1   teaspoon honey

1   to 3 tablespoons milk

- Divide spinach among 4 dinner plates. Arrange cucumber, cabbage, meat, and croutons on top.

- For dressing, stir together mayonnaise, yogurt, mustard, and honey. If necessary, stir in enough milk to make dressing of desired consistency. Spoon dressing over salads. Makes 4 servings.

Smoked Turkey and Pasta Salad

Per serving:
563 cal. (52% from fat), 26 g pro., 43 g carbo., 34 g fat, 75 mg cholesterol, 1 g dietary fiber, 1,012 mg sodium.

**Preparation time:
25 minutes**

**Chilling time:
4 hours**

Vary the ingredients in this salad according to what you have on hand. Use Swiss or cheddar cheese as an option to the Muenster cheese and substitute fully cooked ham for the smoked turkey breast.

1½ cups corkscrew macaroni

6   ounces Muenster cheese, cut into cubes

5   ounces fully cooked smoked turkey breast, cut into bite-size strips

1   small cucumber, coarsely chopped

½   cup coarsely chopped red sweet pepper

2   green onions, sliced

⅓   cup mayonnaise

⅓   cup dairy sour cream

1   tablespoon honey

1   tablespoon Dijon-style mustard

1   to 2 tablespoons milk

Lettuce leaves

- Cook pasta according to package directions. Drain pasta. Rinse with cold water. Drain again.

- Combine cooked pasta, cheese, smoked turkey, cucumber, red pepper, and green onions in a large bowl.

- For dressing, stir together mayonnaise, sour cream, honey, mustard, and ¼ teaspoon *ground black pepper* in a small bowl. Pour dressing over pasta mixture. Toss to coat. Cover and chill for 4 to 24 hours.

- If necessary, stir milk into pasta mixture before serving. Line 4 dinner plates with lettuce leaves. Serve pasta mixture on lettuce-lined plates. Makes 4 servings.

Mexican Orange Roughy Salad

Per serving:
649 cal. (66% from fat), 29 g pro., 28 g carbo., 49 g fat,
67 mg cholesterol, 5 g dietary fiber, 669 mg sodium.

**Preparation time:
15 minutes**

**Chilling time:
2 hours**

**Assembling time:
20 minutes**

Enjoy this updated version of classic Taco Salad. It uses poached fish instead of beef and a creamy dressing instead of salsa.

1   pound fresh or frozen skinless orange roughy

½   cup water

¼   teaspoon salt

¼   cup mayonnaise

¼   cup dairy sour cream

1   jalapeño pepper, seeded and chopped

1   tablespoon milk

1   tablespoon snipped fresh oregano or ½ teaspoon dried oregano, crushed

¼   teaspoon garlic powder

     Several dashes bottled hot pepper sauce

4   cups shredded lettuce

1   large avocado, seeded, peeled, and cut into bite-size pieces

1   cup shredded cheddar or Monterey Jack cheese (4 ounces)

1   cup chopped, seeded tomato

½   cup shredded carrot

⅓   cup sliced pitted ripe olives (optional)

4   purchased tortilla cups or 4 cups tortilla chips

- Thaw fish, if frozen. Cut fish into 1-inch pieces. Combine water and salt in a large skillet. Bring to boiling. Add fish. Return to boiling; reduce heat. Cover and simmer for 3 to 6 minutes or until fish just flakes when tested with a fork. Carefully remove fish from the skillet using a slotted spoon. Cover and refrigerate fish for 2 hours or until well chilled. Discard cooking liquid.

- For dressing, stir together mayonnaise, sour cream, jalapeño pepper, milk, oregano, garlic powder, and bottled hot pepper sauce in a small bowl.

- Combine lettuce, avocado, cheese, tomato, carrot, and, if desired, olives in a large bowl. Toss lightly to mix. Divide the lettuce mixture among the tortilla cups or 4 dinner plates lined with tortilla chips. Top each with some of the fish and dressing. Makes 4 servings.

Handling Hot Peppers

Hot chili peppers, such as jalapeños and serranos, are famous for the fiery kick they add to recipes. But not only do you have to beware when you eat hot chili peppers, you also need to show a little caution when you work with them. Because chili peppers have oils that can burn your skin and eyes, be sure to wear plastic or rubber gloves when you're seeding or chopping the peppers. Also, don't touch or rub your eyes because the oils can irritate them. Finally, once you've finished working with the peppers, wash your hands and nails well with soap and water.

Garden Greens with Swordfish

Garden Greens with Swordfish

Per serving:
288 cal. (57% from fat), 23 g pro., 8 g carbo., 19 g fat,
43 mg cholesterol, 2 g dietary fiber, 354 mg sodium.

**Preparation time:
25 minutes**

The zesty flavor of the
Roasted Pepper Dressing is
the perfect accent for this
sophisticated combination
of swordfish, Belgian
endive, curly endive, and
baby pear tomatoes.

1	pound fresh or frozen swordfish steaks, cut ½ to 1 inch thick
1	tablespoon lemon juice
1	teaspoon dried Italian herb seasoning, crushed
¼	teaspoon garlic salt
⅛	teaspoon pepper
24	small Belgian endive leaves
6	cups torn curly endive
	Roasted Pepper Dressing (see recipe at right)
6	baby pear tomatoes, halved
4	cherry tomatoes, halved
	Fresh herb sprigs

- Thaw fish, if frozen. Brush fish with lemon juice. Combine Italian herb seasoning, garlic salt, and pepper; rub mixture all over fish. Measure thickness of fish. Place fish on the greased, unheated rack of broiler pan.

- Broil 4 inches from the heat until fish just flakes when tested with a fork. Allow 4 to 6 minutes for each ½ inch thickness of fish. (If fish is 1 inch thick, turn halfway through broiling.) Remove fish from rack; cut into strips.

- Divide the Belgian endive leaves and curly endive among 4 dinner plates. Top with fish strips and drizzle with Roasted Pepper Dressing. Trim plates with tomatoes and fresh herb sprigs. Makes 4 servings.

Roasted Pepper Dressing: In a blender container or food processor bowl, combine: 1 large *red sweet pepper*, roasted, or ½ of a 7-ounce jar *roasted sweet peppers*, drained; ¼ cup *salad oil;* 3 tablespoons *white wine vinegar;* ¼ teaspoon *salt;* and dash *ground red pepper*. Cover and blend or process until nearly smooth. Cover and store in the refrigerator for up to 24 hours.

Note: See directions for roasting pepper in Roasted Pepper Salad recipe on page 78.

Cucumber-Dill Cod Salad

Per serving:
265 cal. (60% from fat), 22 g pro., 6 g carbo., 18 g fat,
69 mg cholesterol, 1 g dietary fiber, 437 mg sodium.

**Preparation time:
20 minutes**

**Chilling time:
4 hours**

This tangy salad features
cod. But you'll find that
other kinds of delicately
flavored firm fish, such as
haddock, pike, or pollack,
work just as well.

1	pound fresh or frozen skinless cod, cut into bite-size pieces
½	cup water
½	teaspoon salt
1½	cups chopped seeded cucumber
½	cup dairy sour cream
¼	cup mayonnaise
2	tablespoons snipped fresh dill or 2 teaspoons dried dillweed
2	tablespoons prepared horseradish
1	teaspoon sugar
¼	teaspoon pepper
	Lettuce leaves

- Thaw fish, if frozen. Measure thickness of fish. Combine water and ¼ teaspoon salt in a large skillet; add fish. Bring to boiling; reduce heat. Cover and simmer until fish just flakes when tested with a fork. Allow 4 to 6 minutes for each ½ inch thickness of fish. Drain fish and set aside.

- Stir together the chopped cucumber, sour cream, mayonnaise, dill, horseradish, sugar, remaining ¼ teaspoon salt, and pepper in a large bowl. Gently stir the fish into the cucumber mixture. Cover and chill for 4 to 6 hours.

- To serve, line 4 dinner plates with lettuce leaves. Divide fish mixture among plates. Makes 4 servings.

Warm Tuna and Ginger Salad

Per serving:
235 cal. (36% from fat), 22 g pro., 15 g carbo., 10 g fat,
32 mg cholesterol, 3 g dietary fiber, 153 mg sodium.

**Preparation time:
30 minutes**

Spotting freshness is important when shopping for fish. When buying fresh tuna, look for dark red flesh with a slightly oily sheen. The flesh should spring back and feel firm and elastic when you lightly press it with your finger.

12 ounces fresh or frozen tuna or halibut steaks, cut 1 inch thick

1 teaspoon lemon juice

1 teaspoon soy sauce

1 11-ounce can mandarin orange sections

3 cups coarsely chopped Chinese cabbage

2 cups chopped bok choy

1 cup fresh bean sprouts

1 medium onion, halved

2 teaspoons grated gingerroot

1 clove garlic, minced

1 tablespoon salad oil

2 tablespoons lemon juice

2 tablespoons dry sherry

1 teaspoon toasted sesame oil

2 teaspoons sesame seed, toasted

- Thaw fish, if frozen. Combine the 1 teaspoon lemon juice and the soy sauce; brush on both sides of the tuna or halibut steaks. Place the fish steaks on the greased unheated rack of a broiler pan. Broil 4 inches from the heat for 12 to 16 minutes or until fish just flakes when tested with a fork, turning once. Cut the fish into bite-size pieces.

- Meanwhile, drain mandarin orange sections. Combine the mandarin oranges, Chinese cabbage, bok choy, and bean sprouts in a large bowl. Set aside.

- Slice onion halves. Cook onion, gingerroot, and garlic in hot oil in a medium skillet until onion is tender but not brown, stirring constantly. Remove from heat. Stir the 2 tablespoons lemon juice, the dry sherry, sesame oil, and 2 tablespoons *water* into the onion mixture in the skillet. Heat through. Add fish pieces and onion mixture to cabbage mixture. Toss lightly to mix. Sprinkle with sesame seed. Serve warm. Makes 4 servings.

Salmon-Rigatoni Salad

Per serving:
323 cal. (47% from fat), 16 g pro., 28 g carbo., 17 g fat,
31 mg cholesterol, 1 g dietary fiber, 394 mg sodium.

**Preparation time:
30 minutes**

**Chilling time:
2 hours**

**Assembling time:
15 minutes**

To give this zesty salad a different outlook, make it with mostaccioli or medium-size shell macaroni.

4 ounces rigatoni

3 tablespoons salad oil

3 tablespoons lemon juice

1 teaspoon honey

½ teaspoon dried basil, crushed

1 7½-ounce can salmon, drained

1 small cucumber

4 cups torn salad greens

½ cup crumbled feta cheese

- Cook rigatoni in boiling lightly salted water for 12 to 15 minutes or until *al dente* (tender but still slightly firm). Drain. Rinse with cold water; drain well. For dressing, add oil, lemon juice, honey, basil, and ¼ teaspoon *salt* to the Tupperware® Quick Shake® container. Apply seal and cap; shake well. In a large bowl combine rigatoni and dressing; toss to coat the pasta with dressing. Cover and chill for 2 to 24 hours.

- To serve, remove skin and bones from salmon; break salmon into chunks. Halve cucumber lengthwise; seed halves. Slice cucumber halves. In a salad bowl combine salmon, cucumber, rigatoni with dressing, greens, and feta cheese. Toss lightly. Makes 4 servings.

Dilled Salmon-Potato Salad

Per serving:
583 cal. (60% from fat), 24 g pro., 35 g carbo., 39 g fat,
179 mg cholesterol, 4 g dietary fiber, 412 mg sodium.

Preparation time:
35 minutes

Chilling time:
4 hours

A tangy lemon-dill dressing is tossed with potatoes, salmon, and hard-cooked eggs for this elegant main-dish salad.

3 medium red potatoes

⅔ cup mayonnaise

⅓ cup plain yogurt

1 teaspoon dried dillweed

1 tablespoon milk

½ teaspoon lemon-pepper seasoning

¼ teaspoon garlic powder

1 cup chopped cucumber

¼ cup sliced green onions

1½ cups flaked cooked salmon (8 ounces) or one 15½-ounce can salmon, drained, skin and bones removed, and flaked

2 hard-cooked eggs, chopped

Red-tip leaf lettuce leaves

4 cups shredded red-tip leaf lettuce

- Cut unpeeled potatoes into ¾-inch cubes. Cook potatoes in a covered saucepan in boiling water for 12 to 15 minutes or until just tender. Drain well. Cool slightly.

- For dressing, mix mayonnaise, yogurt, dillweed, milk, lemon-pepper seasoning, and garlic powder in a bowl.

- Combine the dressing, chopped cucumber, and sliced green onions in a large bowl. Add cooked potatoes, the salmon, and the chopped hard-cooked eggs. Toss lightly to mix. Cover and chill for 4 to 24 hours.

- To serve, line 4 dinner plates with lettuce leaves. Top each plate with 1 cup of the shredded lettuce. Divide the salmon mixture among the plates. Makes 4 servings.

Gingerroot Details

The sharp, spicy flavor of gingerroot is the perfect complement to all kinds of salads. Its flavor is hotter and more aromatic than ground ginger. What's more, this knobby root with brown skin and cream-colored flesh is easy to use and store.

When you're at the supermarket, look for a firm piece that's heavy for its size; avoid any pieces with shriveled stems. To keep the gingerroot just a few days, wrap it in a paper towel and refrigerate it. To store it longer, peel and slice the gingerroot. Then cover the slices with sherry or wine and refrigerate them in a covered container for up to 3 months. Or place the unpeeled root in a Tupperware® freezer container and freeze it for up to a year. Grate the amount needed from the frozen root.

Salad Niçoise

Per serving:
392 cal. (46% from fat), 24 g pro., 30 g carbo., 20 g fat,
134 mg cholesterol, 5 g dietary fiber, 82 mg sodium.

Preparation time:
30 minutes

Chilling time:
2 hours

This classic main-dish salad comes from the south of France. Although it usually is made with tuna, you can make this a more colorful entrée by using rosy salmon as shown.

8   ounces green beans

12 ounces whole tiny new potatoes, sliced

¼   cup olive oil or salad oil

¼   cup white wine vinegar or white vinegar

1   teaspoon sugar

1   teaspoon snipped fresh tarragon or ¼ teaspoon dried tarragon, crushed

⅛   teaspoon dry mustard

   Dash pepper

   Boston or Bibb lettuce leaves

1½ cups flaked cooked salmon or tuna (8 ounces) or one 9¼-ounce can chunk white tuna (water pack), drained and broken into chunks

2   medium tomatoes, cut into wedges

2   hard-cooked eggs, cut into wedges

½   cup pitted ripe olives (optional)

¼   cup sliced green onions

8   anchovy fillets, drained, rinsed, and patted dry (optional)

   Fresh chervil (optional)

- Wash green beans. If desired, remove ends and strings. Cook green beans and potatoes in a large covered saucepan or Dutch oven in boiling water for 15 to 20 minutes or until just tender. Drain; place vegetables in a medium bowl. Cover and chill for 2 to 24 hours.

- For dressing, add oil, vinegar, sugar, tarragon, dry mustard, and pepper to the Tupperware® Quick Shake® container. Apply seal and cap; shake well.

- To serve, line 4 dinner plates with lettuce leaves. On the lettuce-lined plates arrange green beans, potatoes, salmon or tuna, tomatoes, hard-cooked eggs, and, if desired, olives. Sprinkle each serving with green onions. If desired, top salads with anchovy fillets and garnish with chervil. Shake dressing well; pour over salads. Makes 4 servings.

Salad Niçoise

Greek-Style Pasta Salad

Per serving:
372 cal. (51% from fat), 18 g pro., 29 g carbo., 21 g fat,
36 mg cholesterol, 2 g dietary fiber, 507 mg sodium.

Preparation time:
30 minutes

Chilling time:
4 hours

The tangy vinaigrette, flavored with mint and oregano, is the perfect accent for the tuna, cucumber, and ripe olives. The dressing tastes great on a simple salad of tossed greens, too.

1	medium cucumber
4	ounces bow-tie macaroni
¼	cup chopped red onion
¼	cup sliced pitted ripe olives
¼	cup salad oil
¼	cup lemon juice
1	teaspoon dried oregano, crushed
½	teaspoon dried mint, crushed
	Lettuce leaves
1	6½-ounce can chunk white tuna (water pack), chilled
1	cup crumbled feta cheese (4 ounces)

- Quarter cucumber lengthwise; seed cucumber and cut into ½-inch-thick slices. Cook pasta according to package directions. Drain pasta. Rinse with cold water. Drain again.

- Combine cooked pasta, cucumber, red onion, and olives in a large bowl. Toss lightly to mix.

- For dressing, add salad oil, lemon juice, oregano, mint, and ¼ teaspoon *pepper* to the Tupperware® Quick Shake® container. Apply seal and cap; shake well. Pour dressing over pasta mixture. Toss well to coat. Cover; chill for 4 to 24 hours.

- Line 4 dinner plates with lettuce. Spoon pasta mixture onto the lettuce-lined plates. Drain tuna and break into chunks. Arrange tuna and feta cheese on top of the pasta mixture. Makes 4 servings.

Shrimp Louis Slaw

Per serving:
351 cal. (64% from fat), 20 g pro., 13 g carbo., 26 g fat,
247 mg cholesterol, 3 g dietary fiber, 468 mg sodium.

Preparation time:
30 minutes

Chilling time:
2 hours

Here's a delicious variation of the classic Louis salad. Tender shrimp and crunchy Chinese cabbage replace the crab and lettuce found in the traditional version.

4	cups water
1	teaspoon salt
12	ounces peeled and deveined shrimp
½	cup mayonnaise
¼	cup sliced green onions
2	tablespoons chili sauce
½	teaspoon finely shredded lemon peel
1	teaspoon lemon juice
1	teaspoon prepared horseradish
4	small tomatoes, thinly sliced
4	cups shredded Chinese cabbage or cabbage
½	cup shredded carrot
2	hard-cooked eggs, cut into wedges

- Bring water and salt to boiling in a large saucepan. Add shrimp. Simmer, uncovered, for 1 to 3 minutes or until shrimp turn pink, stirring occasionally. Drain shrimp and rinse under cold running water. Cover shrimp and chill for 2 to 24 hours.

- For dressing, stir together mayonnaise, green onions, chili sauce, lemon peel, lemon juice, and horseradish in a small bowl. Cover and chill for 2 to 24 hours.

- To serve, arrange tomato slices on 4 dinner plates. Toss together shredded cabbage and shredded carrot; pile on top of tomato slices. Top with chilled shrimp. Arrange egg wedges around each salad. Spoon dressing over salads. Makes 4 servings.

Marinated Shrimp Salad

Per serving:
218 cal. (38% from fat), 21 g pro., 15 g carbo., 10 g fat,
159 mg cholesterol, 5 g dietary fiber, 558 mg sodium.

**Preparation time:
20 minutes**

**Chilling time:
2 hours**

If you have access to fresh herbs, put them to good use in this tangy mustard-herb dressing. Substitute about 1½ teaspoons of snipped fresh herb for every ½ teaspoon of dried herb to give the salad a truly garden-fresh taste.

1¼ pounds fresh shrimp, peeled and deveined

2 6-ounce jars marinated artichoke hearts

2 medium carrots

¾ cup sliced celery

¼ cup sliced green onions

¼ cup sliced pimiento, drained and chopped

2 tablespoons white wine vinegar

1 tablespoon sugar

1 tablespoon salad oil

¾ teaspoon dry mustard

½ teaspoon dried oregano, crushed

½ teaspoon dried basil, crushed

1 clove garlic, minced

½ medium head of red leaf lettuce

- Cook shrimp in boiling water for 2 to 3 minutes or until shrimp turn pink. Drain; cool and chill thoroughly.

- Drain artichoke hearts, reserving marinade. Cut large pieces of artichoke hearts in half. Thinly bias slice carrots. Combine shrimp, artichoke hearts, carrots, celery, green onions, and pimiento in a large bowl.

- For the dressing, add the reserved artichoke marinade, vinegar, sugar, salad oil, mustard, oregano, basil, garlic, and ⅛ teaspoon *pepper* to the Tupperware® Quick Shake® container. Apply seal and cap; shake well. Toss with shrimp mixture. Chill 2 to 24 hours before serving.

- To serve, line serving bowl with red leaf lettuce. Drain dressing from salad, if desired, and transfer salad to serving bowl. Makes 4 servings.

It's All in the Oil

The type of oil you use can make or break a salad dressing. Mild-flavored oils are best for delicate dressings that will be served with mild greens, such as Boston or iceberg lettuce. Strong oils are better in robust dressings to go with hearty greens, such as spinach or radicchio. Here are some common oils used in salads.

Salad or vegetable oils are made from corn, soybeans, canola beans, sunflowers, or peanuts and are mild with little flavor.

Olive oil, a stronger oil, comes in two types. Green olive oil is pressed from semiripe olives and has a sharper taste than golden olive oil, which is made from ripe olives.

Sesame oil is sold in mild and strong versions. The untoasted sesame oil is similar to a vegetable oil with a pale yellow color and mild flavor. Toasted sesame oil is deep brown and has a concentrated flavor. Use it in small amounts.

Nut oils usually are made from walnuts, hazelnuts, or almonds. These oils have delicate flavors and rich aromas.

Seafood Cocktail Salad

Seafood Cocktail Salad

Per serving:
256 cal. (22% from fat), 26 g pro., 26 g carbo., 6 g fat,
185 mg cholesterol, 2 g dietary fiber, 655 mg sodium.

**Preparation time:
20 minutes**

What's the perfect partner for this fruitful twist on classic shrimp cocktail? How about shell-shaped crackers?

⅓ cup Russian Salad Dressing (see recipe, below right)

¼ cup cocktail sauce

8 ounces peeled cooked shrimp

8 ounces coarsely flaked cooked crabmeat

Lettuce leaves

½ of a small honeydew melon, seeded, peeled, and sliced

½ of a small cantaloupe, seeded, peeled, and sliced

1 orange, peeled and sliced crosswise

4 strawberries, halved

- For dressing, stir together Russian Salad Dressing and cocktail sauce. If necessary, stir in a little *water* to make dressing of drizzling consistency. If desired, cover dressing and chill.

- Toss together shrimp, crabmeat, and *3 tablespoons* of the dressing in a medium bowl.

- Arrange lettuce leaves on a serving platter or the Tupperware® Watercolor® Hors D'oeuvre tray. Arrange honeydew and cantaloupe slices, orange slices, and berries on top of lettuce around edge of platter or tray. Spoon seafood mixture onto lettuce in center of platter. Serve with remaining dressing. Garnish with fresh mint, if desired. Makes 6 servings.

Russian Salad Dressing: Add ¼ cup *salad oil*, ¼ cup *catsup*, 1 tablespoon *sugar*, 1 tablespoon *white wine vinegar* or *vinegar*, 1 tablespoon *lemon juice*, 1 teaspoon *Worcestershire sauce*, ½ teaspoon *paprika*, ¼ teaspoon *salt*, and ⅛ teaspoon *pepper* to the Tupperware® Quick Shake® container. Apply seal and cap; shake well. Store in the refrigerator up to 2 weeks. Shake before serving. Makes ⅔ cup (about five 2-tablespoon servings).

Lobster-Melon Salad

Per serving:
348 cal. (37% from fat), 16 g pro., 43 g carbo., 15 g fat,
41 mg cholesterol, 6 g dietary fiber, 375 mg sodium.

**Preparation time:
25 minutes**

The lobster-flavored fish pieces sometimes are called surimi. This "seafood" actually is processed fish that has been flavored and re-formed to look like lobster meat.

1 medium honeydew melon or cantaloupe

6 cups torn romaine

8 ounces coarsely flaked cooked lobster or one 8-ounce package frozen lobster-flavored chunk-style fish pieces, thawed

1 medium papaya, seeded, peeled, and chopped (1½ cups)

2 tablespoons snipped chives

Orange Vinaigrette (see recipe at right)

Lettuce leaves

- Cut honeydew melon or cantaloupe in half and remove the seeds. Use a melon-ball cutter to scoop out pulp (you should have about 3 cups of melon balls).

- Combine melon balls, romaine, lobster, papaya, and chives in a mixing bowl. Pour Orange Vinaigrette over the salad. Toss lightly to coat. Transfer to a lettuce-lined salad bowl. Makes 4 servings.

Orange Vinaigrette: Add ¼ cup *salad oil*, 1 teaspoon finely shredded *orange peel*, ¼ cup *orange juice*, 1 tablespoon *Dijon-style mustard*, and ⅛ teaspoon *pepper* to the Tupperware® Quick Shake® container. Apply seal and cap; shake well.

Spicy Curried Pork Salad

Per serving:
415 cal. (50% from fat), 27 g pro., 29 g carbo., 25 g fat,
50 mg cholesterol, 5 g dietary fiber, 246 mg sodium.

**Preparation time:
45 minutes**

Zesty pork curry becomes a salad when tossed with Chinese cabbage. Regular green or red cabbage are delicious options for the Chinese cabbage.

12	ounces lean boneless pork
3	tablespoons salad oil
3	tablespoons vinegar
1	tablespoon curry powder
1	teaspoon snipped fresh thyme or ¼ teaspoon dried thyme, crushed
1	clove garlic, minced
1	cup bias-sliced celery
1	medium onion, cut into thin wedges
8	cherry tomatoes, halved
½	cup peanuts
½	cup raisins
4	cups coarsely chopped Chinese cabbage

- Trim fat from pork. Partially freeze the pork. Thinly slice across the grain into bite-size pieces. Set pork aside.

- For dressing, add *2 tablespoons* of the oil, the vinegar, curry powder, and thyme to the Tupperware® Quick Shake® container. Apply seal and cap; shake well.

- Pour the remaining 1 tablespoon oil into a wok or large skillet. (Add more oil as necessary during cooking.) Preheat over medium-high heat. Add garlic; stir-fry for 15 seconds. Add celery and onion; stir-fry about 3 minutes or until vegetables are crisp-tender. Remove vegetables from the wok.

- Add the pork to the wok; stir-fry about 3 minutes or until no longer pink. Return vegetables to the work. Shake dressing well. Stir dressing, tomatoes, peanuts, and raisins into pork mixture and heat through.

- Place cabbage in a large salad bowl. Pour pork mixture over the cabbage. Toss lightly to mix. Makes 4 servings.

Pork and Cabbage Salad

Per serving:
386 cal. (54% from fat), 20 g pro., 25 g carbo., 23 g fat,
80 mg cholesterol, 5 g dietary fiber, 300 mg sodium.

**Preparation time:
30 minutes**

**Chilling time:
4 hours**

Croutons make a great addition to this full-flavored pork and vegetable salad. Fix hearty Pumpernickel Croutons (see recipe, page 91) or use your favorite purchased croutons.

2	cups cubed potatoes (3 medium)
4	cups torn leaf lettuce
2	cups shredded red cabbage
8	ounces lean cooked pork roast, cut into bite-size strips (1½ cups)
1	cup frozen peas, thawed
½	cup Thousand Island Dressing (see recipe at right)

- Cook cubed potatoes, covered, in a large saucepan in a small amount of boiling water for 15 to 20 minutes or until tender. Drain potatoes; place in a medium mixing bowl. Cover and chill for 4 to 24 hours.

- To serve, combine leaf lettuce and cabbage in a large salad bowl. Add potatoes, pork, and peas. Toss lightly to mix. Pour dressing over salad. Toss lightly to coat. Makes 4 servings.

Thousand Island Dressing: Stir together 1 cup *mayonnaise* and ¼ cup *chili sauce* in a small bowl. Stir in 1 finely chopped *hard-cooked egg*, 2 tablespoons finely chopped *pimiento-stuffed olives*, 2 tablespoons chopped *green pepper*, 2 tablespoons finely chopped *onion*, and, if desired, 1 teaspoon *Worcestershire sauce*. Cover and store in the refrigerator for up to 1 week. Before serving, if necessary, stir in *milk* to make the dressing the desired consistency. Makes 1½ cups (twelve 2-tablespoon servings).

Prosciutto and Fruit Salad

Per serving:
496 cal. (62% from fat), 19 g pro., 29 g carbo., 36 g fat,
75 mg cholesterol, 4 g dietary fiber, 1,057 mg sodium.

**Preparation time:
25 minutes**

Simplify last-minute meal preparation by assembling, covering, and chilling individual servings of this salad up to 4 hours in advance. Then add the peaches, dressing, and nuts right before serving.

¼ cup whipping cream

½ cup mayonnaise

¼ cup crumbled blue cheese

1 tablespoon milk

½ of a medium cantaloupe, seeded

½ of a medium honeydew melon, seeded

Leaf lettuce

8 ounces thinly sliced prosciutto or fully cooked ham

1 large peach, peeled, pitted, and sliced, or nectarine, pitted and sliced

1 cup strawberries, halved

2 tablespoons coarsely chopped pistachio nuts

• For dressing, whip the cream until soft peaks form in a small bowl. Fold in mayonnaise and blue cheese. If necessary, stir in milk to make dressing of desired consistency. Cover and chill until serving time.

• Scoop pulp out of the cantaloupe and honeydew melon using a melon-ball cutter, as directed in the tip below.

• To serve, line 4 dinner plates with lettuce leaves. Roll up each slice of meat jelly-roll style. Arrange the rolled meat slices on one side of each plate. On the other side of each plate, arrange cantaloupe and honeydew melon balls, peach or nectarine slices, and strawberries. Spoon dressing over the top of each salad. Sprinkle with pistachio nuts. Makes 4 servings.

Melon Ball Magic

Perfectly shaped melon balls make fruit salads look extra special. To cut smooth, round balls, start with a half of a cantaloupe or honeydew melon. Place the cup of a melon-ball cutter, open side down, against the fruit of the melon on one side. Pressing down, twist the melon-ball cutter until the open side of the cup faces up and is full of fruit. Invert the melon-ball cutter into a bowl or onto waxed paper and gently let the melon ball drop out. Positioning the melon-ball cutter as close to the first cut as possible, repeat the cutting motion to form a second melon ball. Continue cutting until you have the amount of melon balls needed.

Cheesy Egg and Greens Toss

Per serving:
173 cal. (54% from fat), 13 g pro., 8 g carbo., 11 g fat,
164 mg cholesterol, 2 g dietary fiber, 448 mg sodium.

**Preparation time:
20 minutes**

When you try this recipe, you'll notice that Swiss chard packs more of a bite than spinach. If Swiss chard is unavailable, however, use all spinach for an equally tasty salad.

1 8-ounce carton plain yogurt

2 to 3 teaspoons prepared horseradish

1 teaspoon sugar

   Dash bottled hot pepper sauce

   Milk

4 cups torn spinach

4 cups torn Swiss chard

4 ounces cheddar cheese, cut into 1-inch-long julienne sticks

1 cup cherry tomatoes, halved

¼ cup sliced green onions

4 hard-cooked eggs, sliced

- For dressing, combine yogurt, horseradish, sugar, hot pepper sauce, and ½ teaspoon *salt* in a small bowl. Stir until well blended. If necessary, stir in enough milk to make dressing of desired consistency. Cover and chill dressing while preparing the salad.

- For salad, combine spinach, Swiss chard, cheddar cheese, tomatoes, and green onions in a large bowl. Toss slightly to mix. Add eggs. Pour dressing over spinach mixture. Toss lightly to coat. Makes 6 servings.

Lentil-Rice Salad

Per serving:
384 cal. (46% from fat), 15 g pro., 37 g carbo., 20 g fat,
30 mg cholesterol, 2 g dietary fiber, 323 mg sodium.

**Preparation time:
40 minutes**

**Chilling time:
2 hours**

This hearty two-grain salad is ideal to make ahead. Just chill it overnight in a Tupperware® 8¾-cup Classic Sheer® Wonderlier® bowl. Then arrange the salad on lettuce-lined plates before serving.

½ cup dry lentils

½ cup long-grain rice

½ cup chopped red or green sweet pepper

⅓ cup shredded carrot

¼ cup sliced green onions

3 tablespoons olive oil

½ teaspoon grated lemon peel

3 tablespoons lemon juice

1½ teaspoons snipped fresh basil

   Lettuce leaves

1 medium tomato, cut into wedges

4 ounces cheddar cheese, sliced

- Rinse and drain lentils. Combine uncooked lentils and 2 cups *water* in a saucepan. Bring to boiling; reduce heat. Simmer, covered, 5 minutes. Add rice. Simmer 15 minutes more. Remove from heat. Let stand, covered, for 10 minutes. Drain. Rinse with cold water. Drain again.

- Combine lentil mixture, red or green pepper, carrot, and green onions. Add oil, lemon peel, lemon juice, basil, and ¼ teaspoon *salt* to the Tupperware® Quick Shake® container. Apply seal and cap; shake well. Pour over lentil mixture; toss. Cover; chill for 2 to 24 hours.

- Line 4 dinner plates with lettuce leaves. Spoon lentil mixture onto lettuce leaves. Top with tomato wedges and cheese slices. Makes 4 servings.

Tortellini and Parsley Pesto Salad

Per serving:
567 cal. (44% from fat), 29 g pro., 52 g carbo., 29 g fat,
83 mg cholesterol, 3 g dietary fiber, 851 mg sodium.

Preparation time:
25 minutes

Chilling time:
4 hours

To add zest to your meals, whip up an extra batch of Parsley Pesto to toss with hot cooked pasta or to top soups and stews. Freeze it in a Tupperware® container for up to a month or refrigerate it for a couple of days. Be sure to bring it to room temperature before serving.

8 ounces broccoli

2 7-ounce packages dried cheese-filled tortellini

Parsley Pesto (see recipe, below)

1 2¼-ounce can sliced pitted ripe olives, drained

6 ounces provolone or mozzarella cheese, cubed

2 medium tomatoes, seeded and chopped

⅓ cup pine nuts, toasted, or ½ cup broken walnuts

- Remove leaves and tough parts of stalks from broccoli. Cut the stalks crosswise into ¼-inch-thick slices, then break flowerets into smaller pieces. (You should have about 2½ cups total.) Set broccoli aside.

- Cook the tortellini according to package directions in a large covered saucepan, adding the broccoli during the last 5 minutes of cooking. Drain.

- Combine broccoli, tortellini, Parsley Pesto, and olives in a large bowl. Toss lightly. Cover; chill for 4 to 24 hours.

- To serve, add provolone or mozzarella cheese, tomatoes, and nuts to the tortellini mixture. Toss lightly to mix. Makes 6 servings.

Parsley Pesto Made Easy

Originally pestos used in Italian cooking were made by "pounding" or "grinding" the herb leaves with a mortar and pestle. Today many cooks simplify the job by using a food processor or blender. See how it's done in this tasty recipe.

Parsley Pesto: Remove the stems from 1¼ ounces of *parsley sprigs.* Measure 1 cup lightly packed parsley. Place the parsley, 2 teaspoons dried *basil,* and 1 clove *garlic* in a food processor bowl or a blender container. Cover and process or blend until the parsley is finely chopped. If necessary, stop the processor or blender and scrape the parsley mixture from the sides of the container. Add ⅓ cup grated *Parmesan* or *Romano cheese.* Cover and process or blend until combined. With lid ajar, add ¼ cup *olive oil* or *salad oil* a little at a time, processing or blending after each addition until well combined.

Fast-Fixing
Supper Salads

When time is short and you need a meal in a hurry, turn to the clever, quick-to-fix entrées featured in this chapter. In about a half an hour, you'll create a great-tasting salad your family will enjoy.

Fruited Chicken and Rice Salad (See recipe, page 51.)

Turkey-Cabbage Salad

Per serving:
424 cal. (68% from fat), 24 g pro., 11 g carbo., 33 g fat,
63 mg cholesterol, 2 g dietary fiber, 1,145 mg sodium.

Preparation time:
15 minutes

Here's an exciting salad for a take-along lunch. Toss the ingredients together the night before and chill in a Tupperware® container. Carry the salad in an insulated lunch box with an ice pack.

¾ cup shredded cabbage

1 small tomato, seeded and chopped

¼ cup cream-style cottage cheese, drained

1 slice turkey breast luncheon meat, cut into 1½-inch-long julienne strips

1 slice (1½ ounces) cheddar cheese, cut into 1½-inch-long julienne strips

2 tablespoons bottled creamy cucumber salad dressing

• Combine cabbage, tomato, cottage cheese, turkey, and cheddar cheese in a small bowl. Toss lightly to mix. Pour creamy cucumber salad dressing over cabbage mixture. Toss lightly to coat.

• Serve immediately or pack as directed at left for a take-along lunch. Makes 1 serving.

Smoked-Turkey Salad

Per serving:
200 cal. (54% from fat), 11 g pro., 13 g carbo., 12 g fat,
26 mg cholesterol, 1 g dietary fiber, 897 mg sodium.

Preparation time:
15 minutes

Flavored with a savory corn-relish dressing, this quick-to-fix salad is perfect for a cool summer supper.

¼ cup mayonnaise

¼ cup plain yogurt

½ cup corn relish

2 cups chopped fully cooked smoked turkey breast

1 stalk celery, thinly sliced

4 lettuce leaves

1 medium tomato, sliced (optional)

• Stir together mayonnaise and yogurt in a medium bowl. Stir in corn relish.

• Add smoked turkey and celery. Toss lightly to coat. Line 4 dinner plates with lettuce leaves. Spoon turkey mixture onto lettuce. If desired, garnish with tomato slices. Makes 4 servings.

Fruited Chicken and Rice Salad

Per serving:
394 cal. (27% from fat), 25 g pro., 48 g carbo., 12 g fat,
54 mg cholesterol, 1 g dietary fiber, 628 mg sodium.

**Preparation time:
35 minutes**

Impress luncheon guests with this sweet and simple entrée. A seasoned rice mix and bottled salad dressing combine deliciously with grapes, canned pineapple, and chicken.

1   6-ounce package long-grain and wild rice mix

1   cup seedless red or green grapes, halved

¼   cup bottled oil-and-vinegar salad dressing

4   medium skinless, boneless chicken breast halves (about ¾ pound total)

½   teaspoon lemon-pepper seasoning

1   8-ounce can pineapple slices (juice pack)

    Spinach (optional)

- Prepare rice mix according to package directions, *except* do not add seasoning mix. Remove from heat; place in a colander and rinse with cold water. Transfer to a bowl. Stir in grapes and seasoning mix.

- Meanwhile, pour *1 tablespoon* of the salad dressing into a large skillet. Add chicken and cook over medium heat 8 to 10 minutes or until tender and no longer pink, turning once. Sprinkle chicken with lemon-pepper. Remove chicken from skillet and cool slightly.

- For dressing, drain pineapple slices, reserving ¼ cup juice. Combine reserved pineapple juice and the remaining salad dressing. Line 4 dinner plates with spinach leaves, if desired. Spoon rice-grape mixture onto plates. Halve pineapple slices. Arrange pineapple and chicken on top of rice mixture. Drizzle dressing over salads. If desired, garnish with fresh herb and lemon peel strips. Makes 4 servings.

Note: Pictured on pages 48–49.

Greek-Style Chicken Salad in Tomato Tulips

Per serving:
269 cal. (55% from fat), 21 g pro., 10 g carbo., 17 g fat,
57 mg cholesterol, 3 g dietary fiber, 498 mg sodium.

**Preparation time:
25 minutes**

Present this robust chicken salad in attractive tomato tulips. Or, to save time, cut the tomatoes into slices and spoon the chicken mixture over the slices.

4   large tomatoes

1½   cups cubed cooked chicken or turkey

½   cup crumbled feta cheese (2 ounces)

½   cup sliced pitted ripe olives

⅓   cup bottled herbs-and-spices salad dressing

    Shredded lettuce

- For tomato tulips, cut out ½ inch of the core from each tomato. Invert tomatoes. Cutting from the top to, but not through, the stem end, cut each tomato into 6 wedges. Set aside.

- Combine chicken, feta cheese, and ripe olives in a medium bowl. Pour herbs-and-spices salad dressing over the chicken mixture. Toss lightly to coat.

- Arrange shredded lettuce on 4 dinner plates. Place tomatoes on top of the lettuce. Spread tomato wedges apart; fill with the chicken mixture. Makes 4 servings.

51

Chicken Waldorf Salad

Per serving:
*428 cal. (53% from fat), 24 g pro., 28 g carbo., 26 g fat,
80 mg cholesterol, 3 g dietary fiber, 482 mg sodium.*

**Preparation time:
5 minutes**

For a salad with show-stopping great looks, select exotic greens such as the mizuna and purple orach used in the photo. But this salad is so flavorful, even when served on plain lettuce it'll still be a great hit.

2   cups chopped cooked chicken (about 10 ounces)

2   cups chopped apple

1   cup thinly sliced celery

1   cup halved seedless red or green grapes

½   cup broken pecans or walnuts

½   cup bottled coleslaw salad dressing

Assorted greens

- Combine chicken, chopped apple, celery, grapes, and pecans or walnuts in a medium bowl. Add the salad dressing and toss lightly to mix. If desired, place in the freezer for 10 minutes to quick-chill or chill up to 4 hours in the refrigerator.

- To serve, line 4 dinner plates with assorted greens and, if desired, top with additional sliced apple. Spoon chicken mixture onto plates. Makes 4 servings.

Turkey and Pepper Salad

Per serving:
*254 cal. (59% from fat), 21 g pro., 6 g carbo., 17 g fat,
55 mg cholesterol, 1 g dietary fiber, 40 mg sodium.*

**Preparation time:
25 minutes**

Serve this simple stir-fried turkey salad with slices of toasty, cheesy bread.

12   ounces turkey breast tenderloin

½   cup bottled oil-and-vinegar salad dressing

3   red, green, and/or yellow sweet peppers, cut into strips

6   cups torn lettuce

- Cut turkey tenderloin into ½-inch-wide strips. Heat ¼ *cup* oil-and-vinegar salad dressing in a 10-inch skillet. Add turkey. Stir-fry over medium-high heat for 3 to 4 minutes or until tender. Remove from heat.

- Add pepper strips to turkey in skillet; stir. Pour the remaining oil-and-vinegar salad dressing over turkey mixture. Toss to coat. Heat through.

- To serve, arrange lettuce on 4 dinner plates. Spoon the turkey mixture over lettuce. Makes 4 servings.

Chicken Waldorf Salad

Tuna and Slaw Salad

Per serving:
271 cal. (24% from fat), 19 g pro., 35 g carbo., 8 g fat,
23 mg cholesterol, 3 g dietary fiber, 391 mg sodium.

**Preparation time:
15 minutes**

Opt for deli-made coleslaw or prepare your own. Either way, you'll enjoy every bite of this quick-to-fix, fruity tuna salad.

2 cups coleslaw

1 9¼-ounce can chunk white tuna (water pack), chilled

1 8-ounce can pineapple chunks (juice pack), chilled and drained

1 cup chopped pear or apple (1 medium)

⅓ cup raisins

   Shredded lettuce

- If coleslaw is very wet, drain off excess liquid. Drain tuna and break into chunks.

- Combine coleslaw, pineapple chunks, chopped pear or apple, and raisins in a medium bowl. Arrange shredded lettuce on 4 dinner plates. Spoon coleslaw mixture into the center of each plate. Make an indentation in the center of each mound of coleslaw mixture; fill with tuna chunks. Makes 4 servings.

Crab-Stuffed Papayas

Per serving:
217 cal. (10% from fat), 21 g pro., 30 g carbo., 3 g fat,
86 mg cholesterol, 8 g dietary fiber, 259 mg sodium.

**Preparation time:
30 minutes**

How do you know when papayas are ripe? Choose fruit that is at least half yellow and feels somewhat soft when you press it.

2 large ripe papayas

   Lemon juice

⅓ cup vanilla yogurt

1 to 2 tablespoons milk

2 cups fresh red raspberries

1 12-ounce package frozen crabmeat, thawed, or two 8-ounce packages frozen crab-flavored salad-style fish, thawed

   Shredded lettuce (optional)

- Halve papayas lengthwise. Scoop out the seeds with a spoon. Remove pulp from centers of papaya halves, leaving ½-inch-thick shells. Peel papayas. Brush insides of shells with lemon juice. Chop enough pulp to measure ½ *cup;* set aside.

- Place vanilla yogurt in a medium bowl. Stir enough of the milk into the yogurt to make dressing of desired consistency. Gently stir in chopped papaya, the raspberries, and crabmeat.

- If desired, arrange shredded lettuce on 4 dinner plates. Spoon crab mixture into papaya shells. Place papaya shells on plates. Makes 4 servings.

Note: If desired, substitute one 10-ounce package frozen red raspberries, thawed, and use 1 to 2 tablespoons of the raspberry juice in place of the milk.

Tangy Salmon Salad

Per serving:
200 cal. (62% from fat), 15 g pro., 4 g carbo., 14 g fat,
8 mg cholesterol, 1 g dietary fiber, 538 mg sodium.

**Preparation time:
10 minutes**

Make this delicious salad even easier by choosing canned salmon that already has the skin and bones removed. Also, use bottled lemon juice instead of squeezing fresh juice.

1	cup sliced celery
½	cup mayonnaise
¼	cup dill pickle relish
2	tablespoons lemon juice
2	7¾-ounce cans salmon, drained, skin and bones removed, and flaked
4	cups shredded lettuce

- Combine celery, mayonnaise, pickle relish, and lemon juice in a medium bowl. Add salmon; toss lightly to coat. If desired, season to taste with pepper. Serve at once or cover and chill to serve later.

- To serve, line 4 dinner plates with shredded lettuce. Spoon salmon mixture onto lettuce. Makes 4 servings.

Italian Tuna Toss

Per serving:
162 cal. (54% from fat), 13 g pro., 6 g carbo., 10 g fat,
14 mg cholesterol, 1 g dietary fiber, 314 mg sodium.

**Preparation time:
15 minutes**

Keep a can of tuna and a few fresh vegetables on hand in the refrigerator so you can enjoy this cool and refreshing meal anytime.

4	cups torn mixed greens
¾	cup halved cherry tomatoes
¾	cup sliced cucumber
1	small onion, thinly sliced and separated into rings
1	6½-ounce can chunk white tuna (water pack), drained and broken into chunks
⅓	cup bottled Italian salad dressing

- Combine torn greens, cherry tomatoes, cucumber slices, and onion rings in a large bowl.

- Add tuna chunks and Italian salad dressing to greens mixture. Toss lightly to coat. Makes 4 servings.

Scouting Out Dressings

Although a salad may start with ingredients low in fat, adding a rich dressing can significantly boost the fat content of the finished dish. For more healthful choices, choose reduced-calorie, low-calorie, no-cholesterol, or fat-free salad dressings at the supermarket. Check the nutrition information on each product so you can choose the one that best fits your needs.

Fish-Avocado Salad

Fish-Avocado Salad

Per serving:
357 cal. (63% from fat), 17 g pro., 17 g carbo., 25 g fat, 38 mg cholesterol, 4 g dietary fiber, 400 mg sodium.

Preparation time: 25 minutes

For a light dinner, serve this elegant fish salad with a slice of crusty French bread and sparkling water.

½ cup water

12 ounces halibut or sea bass, cut 1 inch thick

4 cups torn mixed greens

3 carrots, bias sliced

1 small avocado, seeded, peeled, and cubed

¾ cup bottled Thousand Island salad dressing

- Bring the water to boiling in a skillet. Add the halibut or sea bass. Cover and simmer 8 to 12 minutes or until fish just flakes when tested with a fork. Remove fish; cool slightly and cut into bite-size chunks.

- Toss together torn greens, carrots, and avocado; gently toss in fish chunks. Pile fish and greens mixture in center of each of 4 dinner plates. If desired, arrange red kale leaves and lime slices on the side of each salad. Spoon Thousand Island salad dressing over the salads. If desired, garnish with fresh thyme. Makes 4 servings.

Pork and Vegetable Toss

Per serving:
317 cal. (60% from fat), 22 g pro., 11 g carbo., 22 g fat, 62 mg cholesterol, 3 g dietary fiber, 290 mg sodium.

Preparation time: 30 minutes

A tangy buttermilk dressing complements this garden-fresh vegetable and pork combo.

4 cups torn mixed greens

1 cup shredded red cabbage

8 ounces cooked lean pork roast, cut into bite-size strips

1 cup sliced cauliflower flowerets

1 cup frozen peas, thawed

¾ cup bottled buttermilk salad dressing

- Combine mixed greens and red cabbage in a large bowl. Add pork, cauliflower, and peas. Toss lightly to mix.

- Pour buttermilk salad dressing over salad. Toss lightly to coat. Makes 4 servings.

Beef and Fruit Salad

Per serving:
357 cal. (50% from fat), 24 g pro., 21 g carbo., 21 g fat,
51 mg cholesterol, 4 g dietary fiber, 463 mg sodium.

Preparation time:
20 minutes

Save preparation time by purchasing prewashed fresh spinach. You'll find it in the produce sections of large supermarkets.

1   16-ounce can fruits for salad or tropical fruit salad, chilled

6   cups torn spinach

2   cups cubed cooked lean beef roast

1   medium cucumber, thinly sliced

½   cup bottled poppy seed or creamy cucumber salad dressing

- Drain the chilled fruit. Combine fruit, torn spinach, cubed beef, and sliced cucumber in a large bowl.

- Pour poppy seed or creamy cucumber salad dressing over salad. Toss lightly to coat. Makes 4 servings.

Peppy Taco Salads

Per serving:
340 cal. (59% from fat), 28 g pro., 7 g carbo., 22 g fat,
100 mg cholesterol, 1 g dietary fiber, 509 mg sodium.

Preparation time:
20 minutes

Satisfy your craving for Tex-Mex food in minutes with this salsa-seasoned beef salad. It goes great with tortilla chips.

¾   pound lean ground beef

¾   cup salsa

8   cups torn lettuce or mixed greens

1   cup shredded Monterey Jack cheese with jalapeño peppers or cheddar cheese

¼   cup dairy sour cream or plain yogurt

- Cook ground beef in a medium saucepan until brown. Drain off fat. Stir in salsa and heat through.

- Place lettuce or mixed greens in a large bowl. Spoon meat mixture over lettuce or greens. Sprinkle with shredded cheese. Toss lightly to mix. Top each serving with sour cream or yogurt. Makes 4 servings.

Italian Garbanzo Salad

Per serving:
244 cal. (67% from fat), 9 g pro., 11 g carbo., 18 g fat,
19 mg cholesterol, 2 g dietary fiber, 610 mg sodium.

Preparation time:
15 minutes

Strips of pepperoni and Italian salad dressing add zip to this simple and satisfying salad.

2   ounces pepperoni

½   cup canned garbanzo beans

4   cups torn mixed greens

½   cup shredded provolone or mozzarella cheese

⅓   cup bottled Italian salad dressing

4   mild Italian pickled peppers (optional)

- Cut pepperoni into strips. Rinse and drain the garbanzo beans. Place greens in a large bowl. Add the pepperoni, garbanzo beans, and cheese. Toss lightly to mix.

- Drizzle Italian salad dressing over garbanzo bean mixture. Toss lightly to coat. If desired, add pickled peppers. Makes 4 servings.

Wilted Cabbage Salad with Ham

Per serving:
251 cal. (37% from fat), 23 g pro., 20 g carbo., 11 g fat, 39 mg cholesterol, 8 g dietary fiber, 1,423 mg sodium.

Preparation time: 20 minutes

Stir-fried ham and pepper strips, plus artichokes and celery seed, blend deliciously with cabbage and tomato wedges for this savory salad.

2   6-ounce jars marinated artichoke hearts

2   cups fully cooked ham, cut into julienne strips (10 ounces)

1   large green pepper, cut into thin strips

½   teaspoon celery seed

8   cups torn Chinese cabbage or cabbage

2   medium tomatoes, cut into wedges

Freshly ground black pepper (optional)

- Drain artichokes, reserving marinade. Cut up any large artichoke pieces.

- Heat reserved marinade in a 12-inch skillet over medium-high heat. Add ham and pepper strips. Cook and stir for 2 minutes or until pepper strips are crisp-tender. Add artichokes and celery seed; toss to coat.

- Stir in the cabbage. Cook over medium-high heat about 2 minutes, tossing just until cabbage wilts. Top with tomato wedges. If desired, sprinkle with black pepper. Makes 4 servings.

Lunch on Salads

For a delicious change of pace, pack a light and refreshing salad the next time you head to the office. So your totable salad will stay cool and crisp, follow these pointers:

Start by chilling all food thoroughly before packing.

For tossed salads, carry the ingredients in separate containers and toss the salad just before eating. Tupperware® brand containers are ideal. For example, pack the greens in a 16-ounce One Touch™ Serving Bowl, the dressing in a Classic Sheer® 2-ounce Midget container, and the rest of the salad ingredients in a 6-ounce Little Wonders® container.

For other types of salads, choose a Tupperware container that suits the serving size.

Pack all the items in an insulated bag or cooler with a frozen ice pack. Keep your salad in a cool, dry place until lunchtime.

Spectacular
Side-Dish Salads

These tasty pasta, vegetable, bean, fruit, and gelatin salads make perfect mealtime accompaniments. Rich in color, flavor, and texture, they will entice you to fix salads often.

Garden Salad with Orange Dressing (See recipe, page 62.)

Garden Salad with Orange Dressing

Per serving:
58 cal. (9% from fat), 2 g pro., 13 g carbo., 1 g fat,
0 mg cholesterol, 3 g dietary fiber, 83 mg sodium.

**Preparation time:
25 minutes**

**Chilling time:
2 hours**

The honey-orange dressing gives this pepper, tomato, and summer squash salad irresistible sweetness. Serve it with roasted chicken or turkey and a rice pilaf.

½ teaspoon finely shredded orange peel

3 tablespoons orange juice

2 teaspoons snipped chives

½ teaspoon honey

⅛ teaspoon salt

⅛ teaspoon ground black pepper

2 red sweet peppers, sliced into rings

Lettuce leaves

3 or 4 small red tomatoes, cut into wedges

1 cup yellow pear-shaped tomatoes, halved

3 medium yellow tomatoes, quartered

1 medium yellow summer squash, bias-sliced ¼ inch thick

- For dressing, stir together the orange peel, orange juice, snipped chives, honey, salt, and the black pepper in a small bowl. Set aside.

- Cook red pepper rings in a covered skillet in a small amount of boiling water for 1 to 2 minutes or until crisp-tender; drain and cool. Place pepper rings in a bowl. Add the dressing; toss lightly to coat. Cover and chill for 2 to 24 hours, stirring occasionally.

- To serve, line the Tupperware® Watercolor® Hors D'oeuvre tray or a large platter with lettuce leaves. Drain pepper rings, reserving dressing. Arrange the pepper rings, tomatoes, and squash on tray or platter. Drizzle with the reserved dressing. If desired, garnish with fresh basil. Makes 4 to 6 servings.

Note: Pictured on pages 60–61.

Cottage Cheese and Spinach Salad

Per serving:
125 cal. (38% from fat), 10 g pro., 10 g carbo., 5 g fat,
13 mg cholesterol, 2 g dietary fiber, 383 mg sodium.

**Preparation time:
25 minutes**

Savor this unique blend of cottage cheese and spinach tossed with a creamy horse-radish dressing. A vinegar made with tarragon, chives, or basil creates an out-standing dressing.

½ cup dairy sour cream

2 tablespoons sugar

1 tablespoon prepared horseradish

½ teaspoon dry mustard

¼ teaspoon salt

3 tablespoons herb-flavored vinegar

7 cups torn spinach

1½ cups cottage cheese

½ cup coarsely chopped walnuts (optional)

- For dressing, stir together sour cream, sugar, prepared horseradish, dry mustard, and salt in a small bowl. Gradually mix in the herb-flavored vinegar using a wire whisk. Cover and chill until serving time.

- To serve, place the torn spinach in a large bowl. Spoon the cottage cheese on top of the spinach in a ring. If desired, sprinkle with the walnuts. Pour dressing over salad. Toss lightly to coat. Makes 6 to 8 servings.

Honey-Mustard Slaw

Per serving:
294 cal. (75% from fat), 4 g pro., 16 g carbo., 26 g fat,
19 mg cholesterol, 3 g dietary fiber, 203 mg sodium.

**Preparation time:
15 minutes**

Here's an interesting new twist on classic coleslaw. It combines cabbage with shredded romaine and jicama, then everything is tossed with a tangy sour cream and mayonnaise dressing.

½ cup mayonnaise

½ cup dairy sour cream

2 tablespoons honey

1 to 2 tablespoons Dijon-style or coarse-grain brown mustard

3 cups coarsely shredded cabbage

2 cups coarsely shredded romaine

1 small jicama, peeled and shredded (2 cups)

¼ cup sliced green onions

Romaine leaves (optional)

½ cup toasted broken pecans

- For dressing, stir together mayonnaise, sour cream, honey, and mustard in a small bowl. Cover and chill.

- Combine shredded cabbage, shredded romaine, jicama, and green onions in a large bowl. Cover and chill.

- To serve, add dressing to cabbage mixture. Toss lightly to coat. If desired, serve in a romaine-lined bowl. Sprinkle with pecans. Makes 6 servings.

Toasting Tips

Toasted almonds, pecans, walnuts, and sesame seed lend a wonderfully nutty flavor and crunchy texture to salads. You can easily toast a big batch of nuts to store in the freezer and add to salads whenever you like. To toast nuts or sesame seed, spread in a thin layer in a shallow ungreased baking pan. Bake in a 350° oven for 5 to 10 minutes, or until light golden brown, stirring once or twice and checking often to keep from burning. Cool the toasted nuts or sesame seed before using or storing.

Ruffled Pasta in Wilted Greens

Per serving:
115 cal. (33% from fat), 3 g pro., 16 g carbo., 4 g fat,
0 mg cholesterol, 1 g dietary fiber, 263 mg sodium.

Preparation time:
25 minutes

Turn to this flavorful salad when you need a dish to complement a plain entrée, such as broiled chops. Its Oriental-style seasonings, ruffled pasta, and wilted greens will add just the right accent.

2   cups tricolor pasta ruffles or corkscrew macaroni (4 ounces)

2   tablespoons water

2   tablespoons dry sherry

2   tablespoons soy sauce

1   tablespoon honey

1   tablespoon lemon juice

1   large red onion, thinly sliced and separated into rings

1   tablespoon sesame seed

2   tablespoons sesame oil or salad oil

6   cups torn mixed greens

- Cook pasta according to package directions. Drain pasta. Rinse with cold water; drain again. Set aside.

- Meanwhile, add the 2 tablespoons water, the dry sherry, soy sauce, honey, and lemon juice to the Tupperware® Quick Shake® container. Apply seal and cap; shake well. Set aside.

- Cook onion rings and sesame seed in a large skillet in hot oil about 5 minutes or just until onion is tender and sesame seed is toasted. Stir in soy mixture; bring to boiling. Remove from heat. Add cooked pasta. Toss lightly to coat.

- Place greens in a large bowl. Pour pasta mixture over greens. Toss lightly to mix. Makes 8 servings.

Carrot-Raisin Salad

Per serving:
136 cal. (62% from fat), 1 g pro., 13 g carbo., 10 g fat,
7 mg cholesterol, 2 g dietary fiber, 81 mg sodium.

Preparation time:
15 minutes

Chilling time:
2 hours

Now you can make this ever-popular restaurant salad-bar favorite at home. The raisins and apple naturally sweeten the carrot mixture.

3   medium carrots, shredded

1   small apple, chopped (¾ cup)

⅓   cup raisins

1   teaspoon lemon juice

⅓   cup mayonnaise

1   to 2 tablespoons milk

¼   cup toasted slivered almonds (optional)

- Combine carrots, apple, and raisins in a medium bowl. Sprinkle with lemon juice. Add mayonnaise. Toss lightly to coat. Cover and chill for 2 to 24 hours.

- To serve, if dressing becomes too thick, stir in milk. If desired, sprinkle with almonds. Makes 6 servings.

Ruffled Pasta in Wilted Greens

Orange and Avocado Salad

Per serving:
190 cal. (79% from fat), 2 g pro., 9 g carbo., 17 g fat,
11 mg cholesterol, 2 g dietary fiber, 201 mg sodium.

**Preparation time:
30 minutes**

The sophisticated flavor of
the Tarragon Dressing
brings out the best in this
salad. If you like, use fresh
mandarin oranges or
tangerines in place of the
canned ones. Look for them
from October to April.
When you find them, peel
and section two or three,
and add to the salad.

4   cups torn mixed greens

1   11-ounce can mandarin
orange sections,
drained

1   cup sliced fresh
mushrooms

½   of a medium avocado,
seeded, peeled, and
cubed

½   cup shredded carrot

Tarragon Dressing (see
recipe, above right)

¼   cup slivered almonds
or pine nuts, toasted
(optional)

- Combine torn mixed greens, mandarin orange sections,
mushrooms, avocado, and shredded carrot in a large
bowl. Pour Tarragon Dressing over salad. Toss lightly to
coat. If desired, sprinkle with almonds or pine nuts.
Makes 6 to 8 servings.

Tarragon Dressing: In a small bowl stir together:
½ cup *mayonnaise;* 2 tablespoons *lemon juice* or *vinegar;*
2 teaspoons snipped *fresh tarragon* or ½ teaspoon *dried
tarragon,* crushed; 1½ teaspoons *soy sauce;* ¼ teaspoon
pepper; and 1 clove *garlic,* minced. If desired, cover and
chill the dressing.

Garden Greens with Blueberry Dressing

Per serving:
151 cal. (47% from fat), 3 g pro., 19 g carbo., 8 g fat,
1 mg cholesterol, 3 g dietary fiber, 107 mg sodium.

**Preparation time:
20 minutes**

**Chilling time:
1 hour**

Blueberries star in the
sweet, yet tart, vinaigrette
dressing of this savory
vegetable and fruit salad.

4   cups torn mixed greens

1   cup sliced fresh
mushrooms

2   medium apples, cored
and sliced

½   cup Parmesan Croutons
(see recipe, page 91)

½   cup Blueberry Dressing
(see recipe at right)

- Combine torn mixed greens and the mushrooms in a
large bowl. Toss lightly to mix. Divide the mixture
among 4 salad plates. Top each plate with apple slices
and Parmesan Croutons.

- Shake Blueberry Dressing well; pour *2 tablespoons* of
the dressing over each salad. If desired, garnish with
fresh basil. Makes 4 servings.

Blueberry Dressing: Combine ½ cup fresh or frozen
blueberries (thaw blueberries, if frozen), ¼ cup *white
wine vinegar,* ½ teaspoon *sugar,* ⅛ teaspoon *pepper,* and
dash *salt* in a blender container or food processor bowl.
Cover and blend or process until the berries are puréed.
Sieve the mixture to remove the skins; discard the skins.
To a Tupperware® Quick Shake® container, add the
blueberry mixture, 3 tablespoons *salad oil,* and 2
teaspoons snipped *fresh basil* or ½ teaspoon *dried basil,*
crushed. Apply seal and cap; shake well. Chill at least 1
hour. Refrigerate remaining dressing for up to 2 weeks.
Makes about 1⅓ cups (ten 2-tablespoon servings).

Spring Greens Salad

Per serving:
63 cal. (67% from fat), 1 g pro., 4 g carbo., 5 g fat,
5 mg cholesterol, 1 g dietary fiber, 54 mg sodium.

Preparation time:
15 minutes

Chilling time:
1 hour

Tender greens, crisp vegetables, and a fragrant herb dressing create this crowd-pleasing salad. Serve this in the Tupperware® 6-quart Watercolor® salad bowl.

10	cups torn mixed greens
2	small tomatoes, cut into thin wedges
2	medium carrots, thinly bias sliced
1	cup sliced fresh mushrooms
⅓	cup loosely packed parsley sprigs
¼	cup mayonnaise
¼	cup dairy sour cream or plain yogurt
2	tablespoons milk
1	teaspoon Dijon-style mustard
3	tablespoons snipped chives

- Combine mixed greens, tomato wedges, carrots, and mushrooms in a large bowl. Toss lightly to mix. Cover and chill for 1 to 8 hours.

- For dressing, combine parsley, mayonnaise, sour cream or yogurt, milk, and mustard in a blender container or food processor bowl. Cover and blend or process until mixture is combined. Stir in snipped chives.

- To serve, pour the dressing over the greens mixture. Toss lightly to coat. Makes 12 servings.

Timesaving Greens

If you don't want to keep several kinds of greens or vegetables on hand for a salad, then check out the innovative salad mixtures in your supermarket produce department. They are ready to use and often are cheaper than buying several types of whole greens or vegetables that would result in lots of leftovers. The most commonly available salad mixtures include:

Broccoli slaw: shredded broccoli mixed with shredded carrot.

Classic-style mix: a combination of torn iceberg lettuce, shredded carrot, and shredded red cabbage.

Coleslaw mix: shredded cabbage teamed with shredded carrot.

French-style mix: torn butter and iceberg lettuces tossed with shredded carrot and shredded red cabbage.

Italian-style mix: torn romaine and torn radicchio; sometimes mixed with other vegetables.

Other mixtures: other combinations may be available in your area (for example, a blend of five torn greens such as iceberg lettuce, romaine, escarole, endive, and radicchio).

Warm Potato and Squash Salad

Layered 24-Hour Salad

Per serving:
245 cal. (78% from fat), 6 g pro., 7 g carbo., 22 g fat,
91 mg cholesterol, 2 g dietary fiber, 262 mg sodium.

**Preparation time:
40 minutes**

**Chilling time:
4 hours**

Here's the perfect salad choice for a potluck. The layers of ingredients stay crisp and fresh until serving time.

6	slices bacon
2	small tomatoes
4	cups torn mixed greens
1	cup sliced fresh mushrooms
1	cup shredded carrot
½	cup thinly sliced celery
½	cup sliced radishes
2	hard-cooked eggs, sliced
¼	cup sliced green onions
	Buttermilk-Herb Dressing (see recipe at right)
¾	cup shredded cheddar cheese (optional)

- Cook bacon in a skillet until crisp; drain and crumble. Cut tomatoes into thin wedges. Place greens in the bottom of a 3-quart bowl. Layer in the following order: mushrooms, tomato wedges, carrot, celery, radishes, egg slices, bacon, and green onions.

- Spread Buttermilk-Herb Dressing evenly over the top of the salad, covering to the edge of the bowl. If desired, sprinkle with cheese. Cover and chill for 4 to 24 hours. To serve, toss lightly to mix. Makes 6 to 8 servings.

Buttermilk-Herb Dressing: In a small bowl stir together: ½ cup *mayonnaise;* ¼ cup *dairy sour cream;* 2 tablespoons *buttermilk;* 1 tablespoon snipped *fresh basil* or 1 teaspoon *dried basil,* crushed; 1 tablespoon snipped *parsley;* ¼ teaspoon *pepper;* ¼ teaspoon *garlic powder;* and ¼ teaspoon *onion powder.*

Warm Potato and Squash Salad

Per serving:
338 cal. (59% from fat), 6 g pro., 30 g carbo., 23 g fat,
0 mg cholesterol, 4 g dietary fiber, 40 mg sodium.

**Preparation time:
30 minutes**

New potatoes, cherry tomatoes, yellow summer squash, and an herbed vinaigrette make this potato salad extraordinary. Garnish with a bundle of fresh tarragon and chives tied with a chive stem.

¾	pound whole tiny new potatoes, cut up
1	cup cherry tomatoes
1	small yellow summer squash
½	cup broken walnuts
¼	cup sliced green onions
¼	cup salad oil
3	tablespoons white wine vinegar or vinegar
1½	teaspoons sugar
1	teaspoon dried tarragon, crushed
1	teaspoon snipped chives
½	teaspoon Dijon-style mustard
	Romaine leaves

- Cook new potatoes in a covered saucepan in boiling salted water for 12 to 15 minutes or until just tender; drain well. Halve cherry tomatoes. Cut yellow summer squash into bite-size strips.

- Mix cooked potatoes, cherry tomatoes, yellow summer squash, walnuts, and green onions in a large bowl.

- For dressing, add the salad oil, vinegar, sugar, tarragon, snipped chives, mustard, and dash *pepper* to the Tupperware® Quick Shake® container. Apply seal and cap; shake well. Pour the dressing over the potato mixture. Toss lightly to coat.

- Line 4 salad plates with romaine leaves. Divide the potato mixture among the romaine-lined plates. If desired, garnish with chive-tarragon bundles. Serves 4.

Tarragon Bean Salad

Per serving:
222 cal. (32% from fat), 7 g pro., 32 g carbo., 8 g fat,
0 mg cholesterol, 9 g dietary fiber, 441 mg sodium.

Preparation time:
25 minutes

Chilling time:
4 hours

Chill this tangy two-bean combo no more than the recommended time before serving to keep the snap beans at their brightest. When fresh beans are out of season, substitute frozen cut green beans cooked according to package directions.

3	cups green and/or yellow snap beans
2	tablespoons vinegar
2	tablespoons salad oil
1	shallot, finely chopped
2	teaspoons snipped fresh tarragon or ¼ teaspoon dried tarragon, crushed
1	teaspoon sugar
½	teaspoon dry mustard
¼	teaspoon salt
1	15-ounce can garbanzo beans, drained
1	medium tomato, coarsely chopped

- Bias-slice snap beans into 1½-inch lengths. Place a steamer basket in a saucepan; add water until it almost touches the bottom of the steamer basket. Add the snap beans and steam for 18 to 22 minutes or until the beans are crisp-tender; drain.

- Meanwhile, for dressing, add the vinegar, salad oil, shallot, tarragon, sugar, dry mustard, and salt to the Tupperware® Quick Shake® container. Apply seal and cap; shake well.

- Combine the cooked beans, garbanzo beans, and tomato in a large bowl. Add the dressing; toss lightly to coat. Cover and chill about 4 hours, stirring once. Serve using a slotted spoon. Makes 4 servings.

Spinach and Pasta Salad

Per serving:
297 cal. (37% from fat), 10 g pro., 37 g carbo., 12 g fat,
15 mg cholesterol, 2 g dietary fiber, 116 mg sodium.

Preparation time:
25 minutes

Chilling time:
4 hours

White wine vinegar, basil, and oregano give this contemporary pasta salad a taste of old Italy. Serve it with grilled beef steaks or burgers.

1½	cups corkscrew macaroni (4 ounces)
1	medium red, yellow, or green sweet pepper, cut into bite-size pieces
½	cup chopped onion
½	cup cubed cheddar cheese (2 ounces)
2	tablespoons salad oil
2	tablespoons white wine vinegar or white vinegar
1	teaspoon snipped fresh basil or ¼ teaspoon dried basil, crushed
1	teaspoon snipped fresh oregano or ¼ teaspoon dried oregano, crushed
½	teaspoon pepper
2	cups torn spinach

- Cook pasta according to package directions. Drain pasta. Rinse with cold water; drain again.

- Combine cooked pasta, the sweet pepper, onion, and cheddar cheese in a large bowl.

- For dressing, add the salad oil, white wine vinegar, basil, oregano, and pepper to the Tupperware Quick Shake® container. Apply seal and cap; shake well. Pour dressing over pasta mixture. Toss to coat. Cover; chill for 4 to 24 hours.

- To serve, toss the torn spinach with the pasta mixture. Makes 4 or 5 servings.

Oriental Cabbage Salad

Per serving:
279 cal. (54% from fat), 7 g pro., 28 g carbo., 18 g fat,
0 mg cholesterol, 6 g dietary fiber, 529 mg sodium.

Preparation time:
15 minutes

Chilling time:
4 hours

The package of ramen noodles contributes both the crunchy noodles for the salad and the seasonings for the tasty dressing. To keep the noodles crisp, add them to the salad just before serving.

1	3-ounce package chicken-flavored ramen noodles
¼	cup salad oil
¼	cup rice vinegar or white wine vinegar
1	tablespoon sugar
¼	teaspoon pepper
1	8¾-ounce can baby corn, drained
2	cups shredded red and/or green cabbage
1	cup fresh pea pods
1	7-ounce jar whole straw mushrooms, drained
¼	cup sliced green onions
	Chinese cabbage leaves
2	teaspoons sesame seed, toasted (optional)
4	radishes, halved lengthwise (optional)

- For dressing, add the seasoning packet from the ramen noodles, salad oil, vinegar, sugar, and pepper to the Tupperware® Quick Shake® container. Apply seal and cap; shake well to dissolve seasonings.

- Cut each ear of baby corn crosswise in half. Combine baby corn, cabbage, pea pods, straw mushrooms, and green onions in a large bowl. Shake dressing well; pour over cabbage mixture. Toss lightly to coat. Cover and chill for 4 to 24 hours.

- To serve, break dry Oriental noodles into pieces. Add noodles to cabbage mixture; toss lightly to mix. Line 4 salad plates with cabbage leaves. Divide cabbage mixture among the cabbage-lined plates. If desired, sprinkle each serving with toasted sesame seed and garnish with radishes. Makes 4 servings.

Great-Tasting Vinegars

When it comes to adding pizzaz to vinegar-based salad dressings, you can choose from dozens of vinegar options. To help sort out all of the varieties, colors, and flavors, here is a brief description of some of the most common vinegar types.

Balsamic: a dark brown vinegar made from sweet grapes with a slightly sweet, delicate flavor.

Cider: a golden brown vinegar made from apples with a strong bite and a faint apple flavor.

Fruit: a vinegar made with cider, white, or white wine vinegar and a fruit, such as raspberries, strawberries, or lemons.

Herb: a cider, white, or wine vinegar with an added herb, such as basil, tarragon, thyme, mint, or dill.

Rice: a vinegar used in Oriental cooking that is made from rice wine or sake. It is clear or pale gold with a slightly sweet tang.

White: a sharp, clear vinegar based on grain alcohol.

Wine: a vinegar made from sherry, champagne, or white, red, or rosé wine. The color and flavor depend on the wine used.

Cranberry Soufflé Salad

Per serving:
299 cal. (49% from fat), 2 g pro., 37 g carbo., 17 g fat,
61 mg cholesterol, 2 g dietary fiber, 48 mg sodium.

Preparation time:
55 minutes

Chilling time:
4 hours

To make the sugar-coated cranberries shown on this festive gelatin salad, brush cranberries with light corn syrup and then roll in sugar until coated.

2½ cups orange juice

1   16-ounce can whole cranberry sauce

1   6-ounce package raspberry-flavored gelatin

1½ cups whipping cream

    Orange chunks

    Sugar-coated cranberries (optional)

● Mix *1¼ cups* of the orange juice, cranberry sauce, and raspberry-flavored gelatin in a medium saucepan. Cook and stir over medium heat until the gelatin is dissolved. Stir in the remaining orange juice. Chill until mixture is partially set (consistency of unbeaten egg whites).

● Beat whipping cream in a small bowl until soft peaks form. Fold into the gelatin mixture. Chill until the mixture mounds. Pour into the Tupperware® Jel-Ring® mold. Chill for 4 to 6 hours or until firm.

● To serve, unmold the salad. Fill center of the salad with orange chunks and, if desired, sugar-coated cranberries. If desired, garnish with orange leaves. Serves 8 to 10.

Note: To unmold the salad, immerse the Jel-Ring mold into warm water for 20 to 30 seconds. Remove the large seal, turn a serving plate upside down and center over the mold, then invert the plate and mold together. Carefully lift off the center seal and the mold.

Strawberries and Cream Gelatin Salad

Per serving:
149 cal. (31% from fat), 2 g pro., 25 g carbo., 5 g fat, 11 mg
cholesterol, 1 g dietary fiber, 25 mg sodium.

Preparation time:
1¼ hours

Chilling time:
6 hours

Filled with fruit and flavored with sour cream, this two-layer salad creation can double as a dessert. Just serve it on fancy china dessert plates without the lettuce.

1   10-ounce package frozen sliced strawberries, thawed

1   cup apple juice

1   3-ounce package strawberry-flavored gelatin

1   8¼-ounce can crushed pineapple

¼   cup sugar

1   envelope unflavored gelatin

1   8-ounce carton dairy sour cream

½   teaspoon finely shredded lemon peel

1   tablespoon lemon juice

    Lettuce leaves

● Drain the strawberries, reserving juice; set aside. Bring *¾ cup* of the apple juice to boiling in a medium saucepan; remove from heat. Add gelatin, stirring until dissolved. Stir in the remaining apple juice and the reserved strawberry juice. Chill until the mixture is partially set (the consistency of unbeaten egg whites).

● Stir strawberries into the partially set gelatin. Pour mixture into a 9x9x2-inch pan or a Tupperware® Cold Cut Keeper. Chill until almost firm (mixture appears set, but will flow if tipped).

● Meanwhile, drain pineapple, reserving juice; set aside. Combine sugar, unflavored gelatin, and ½ cup *water* in a medium saucepan. Let stand 5 minutes to soften. Cook and stir over medium heat until gelatin is dissolved. Stir in the reserved pineapple juice, sour cream, lemon peel, lemon juice, and ¼ cup *water*. Beat with a rotary beater until smooth. Chill until partially set (the consistency of unbeaten egg whites). Stir pineapple into partially set gelatin. Pour over the strawberry layer. Chill for at least 6 hours or until firm.

● To serve, line 9 salad plates with lettuce leaves. Cut the salad into squares; serve on plates. Makes 9 servings.

Cranberry Soufflé Salad

Brown Rice and Vegetable Salad

Per serving:
153 cal. (43% from fat), 3 g pro., 20 g carbo., 8 g fat,
0 mg cholesterol, 3 g dietary fiber, 85 mg sodium.

Preparation time:
50 minutes

Chilling time:
4 hours

If you like the texture and the slightly nutty flavor that the brown rice adds to this salad, consider substituting it for white rice in other salads.

1½ cups cooked brown rice

1¼ cups coarsely chopped, seeded tomato

2 medium carrots, cut into julienne strips

½ cup frozen peas

¼ cup sliced green onions

1 tablespoon snipped parsley

1 tablespoon snipped fresh dill or 1 teaspoon dried dillweed

Summer Vinaigrette (see recipe, above right)

Lettuce leaves

- Stir together cooked brown rice, chopped tomato, carrot strips, peas, green onions, parsley, and dill in a large bowl. Pour Summer Vinaigrette over the rice mixture. Toss lightly to coat. Cover and chill for 4 to 24 hours.

- To serve, line a large bowl with lettuce leaves. Spoon the salad into the lettuce-lined bowl. Makes 6 servings.

- **Summer Vinaigrette:** To the Tupperware® Quick Shake® container, add 3 tablespoons *olive oil* or *salad oil*, 3 tablespoons *red wine vinegar*, 2 teaspoons *Dijon-style mustard*, 1½ teaspoons *sugar*, and ⅛ teaspoon pepper. Apply seal and cap; shake well.

Red-Pepper Two-Grain Salad

Per serving:
201 cal. (46% from fat), 4 g pro., 25 g carbo., 11 g fat,
0 mg cholesterol, 5 g dietary fiber, 217 mg sodium.

Preparation time:
30 minutes

Chilling time:
4 hours

Crushed red pepper gives this bulgur-couscous salad hotness that builds with each forkful. Serve it with grilled or broiled chicken or fish.

2 cups water

½ cup bulgur

½ cup couscous

1 2¼-ounce can (⅔ cup) sliced pitted ripe olives, drained

½ cup shredded carrot

¼ cup sliced green onions

¼ cup olive oil or salad oil

½ teaspoon finely shredded lime peel

¼ cup lime juice

2 teaspoons sugar

½ to 1 teaspoon crushed red pepper

¼ teaspoon salt

Radicchio and/or white salad savoy leaves

- Combine water and bulgur in a medium saucepan. Bring to boiling; reduce heat. Cover and simmer for 10 to 15 minutes or until bulgur is almost tender. Remove from heat; stir in the couscous. Let mixture stand, covered, for 5 minutes. Drain. Rinse with cold water; drain again.

- Combine the cooked grain mixture, olives, shredded carrot, and sliced green onions in a large bowl.

- For dressing, add the olive oil or salad oil, lime peel, lime juice, sugar, red pepper, and salt to the Tupperware Quick Shake® container. Apply seal and cap; shake well. Pour dressing over salad mixture. Toss lightly to coat. Cover and chill for 4 to 24 hours.

- To serve, line salad plates with radicchio and/or white salad savoy leaves. Divide salad mixture among plates. If desired, garnish each serving with julienne strips of carrot and a green onion curl. Makes 6 to 8 servings.

Yellow Rice and Avocado Salad

Per serving:
284 cal. (61% from fat), 8 g pro., 21 g carbo., 20 g fat, 79 mg cholesterol, 2 g dietary fiber, 490 mg sodium.

**Preparation time:
30 minutes**

**Chilling time:
2 hours**

Saffron-flavored rice and tongue-tingling Lemon Dressing make this salad special enough to be invited to your next dinner party.

½ cup long-grain rice

½ teaspoon salt

⅛ teaspoon ground saffron or ground turmeric

Lemon Dressing (see recipe, below right)

3 cups torn romaine

3 cups torn red-tip leaf lettuce

4 slices Swiss cheese, cut into julienne strips (2 ounces)

1 large avocado, seeded, peeled, and sliced

1 medium tomato, thinly sliced

2 hard-cooked eggs, sliced

- Cook rice according to package directions, *except* add the salt and saffron or turmeric. Cool rice slightly. Combine rice and *2 tablespoons* of the Lemon Dressing. Cover and chill for 2 to 24 hours. Cover and chill remaining dressing for 2 to 24 hours.

- To serve, combine torn romaine and leaf lettuce in a large bowl. Mound the cooked rice in the center. Arrange cheese strips, avocado, tomato, and egg slices around rice. Shake dressing well; pour over the salad. Toss lightly to coat. Makes 6 to 8 servings.

Lemon Dressing: To the Tupperware Quick Shake® container, add ¼ cup *olive* or *salad oil*, ¼ cup *water*, 3 tablespoons *lemon juice*, 1 tablespoon *Dijon-style mustard*, 1 teaspoon *sugar*, ½ teaspoon *salt*, and ⅛ teaspoon *pepper*. Apply seal and cap; shake well.

Soup and Salad Buffet

Think salad when you need a change-of-pace idea for a luncheon or dinner party. With a little planning, you can offer your guests a choice of several main-dish salads, a soup, and piping-hot rolls or muffins, all served buffet-style.

Start by planning your menu, remembering to keep the number of recipes manageable. You'll want to choose salads that offer variety. For example, team a tossed chef's-type salad with a vinaigrette-based pasta salad, and, perhaps, a creamy chicken or seafood salad. Then add a soup that complements the salads. If you're serving several creamy salads, choose a broth-based soup. If not, a cream or cheese soup will work fine. Finally choose one or two breads to go with the buffet. Muffins, bread-sticks, or rolls are handy because they don't have to be sliced.

On party day, keep last-minute preparation to a minimum. If possible, make the soup and breads a day or two in advance and prepare the salads several hours ahead. Make dessert easy by serving ice cream and your favorite bakery cookies.

Pear Salad with Orange Dressing

Pear Salad with Orange Dressing

Per serving:
180 cal. (27% from fat), 4 g pro., 32 g carbo., 6 g fat,
2 mg cholesterol, 5 g dietary fiber, 25 mg sodium.

**Preparation time:
20 minutes**

This refreshing dressing made with yogurt and orange juice and peel brings out the wonderful flavor of juicy, ripe pears in this salad. Another time, use peaches or nectarines in place of the pears.

¼	teaspoon finely shredded orange peel (set aside)
2	oranges
½	cup vanilla yogurt
1	tablespoon honey
4	cups torn mixed greens
2	medium pears, cored and sliced
¼	cup chopped pecans

- Peel oranges. Working over a bowl to catch the juices, section the oranges; set sections aside. Measure and reserve *1 tablespoon* of the orange juice.

- For dressing, combine the reserved orange juice, the orange peel, vanilla yogurt, and honey.

- Place torn mixed greens in the Tupperware® 6-cup serving bowl. Arrange orange sections and pear slices on top of the greens. Drizzle the dressing over the fruit and greens. Sprinkle salad with chopped pecans. If desired, garnish with strips of orange peel and whole pecans. Makes 4 servings.

Five-Cup Salad

Per serving:
223 cal. (53% from fat), 2 g pro., 25 g carbo., 14 g fat,
17 mg cholesterol, 2 g dietary fiber, 30 mg sodium.

**Preparation time:
10 minutes**

**Chilling time:
2 hours**

This rich-tasting fruit and coconut salad is a long-standing potluck and buffet favorite. Its name comes from the fact that the recipe often uses one cup each of five ingredients to create the salad. In our version, the crunchy chopped pecans are a bonus.

1	8¼-ounce can pineapple chunks
1	11-ounce can mandarin orange sections, drained
1	cup coconut
1	cup tiny marshmallows
1	8-ounce carton dairy sour cream
2	tablespoons chopped pecans

- Drain pineapple chunks, reserving *1 tablespoon* of the syrup. Combine pineapple chunks, reserved syrup, mandarin orange sections, coconut, marshmallows, and sour cream in a medium bowl. Cover the fruit mixture and chill for 2 to 24 hours.

- To serve, sprinkle salad with pecans. Makes 6 servings.

Roasted Pepper Salad

Per serving:
96 cal. (61% from fat), 2 g pro., 8 g carbo., 7 g fat,
0 mg cholesterol, 2 g dietary fiber, 78 mg sodium.

Preparation time:
50 minutes

Chilling time:
4 hours

Baby pear tomatoes and red and yellow sweet peppers team for strikingly colorful results in this salad. For variety, use artichoke hearts instead of the hearts of palm.

2	medium red and/or yellow sweet peppers
1	medium green pepper
1	cup broccoli flowerets
1	cup baby pear tomatoes or cherry tomatoes, halved
½	cup sliced canned hearts of palm, drained
2	tablespoons salad oil
1	tablespoon snipped parsley
1	tablespoon water
1	tablespoon lemon juice
2	cloves garlic, minced
1	teaspoon dried basil, crushed
⅛	teaspoon salt
⅛	teaspoon ground black pepper
	Boston lettuce leaves

- To roast peppers, quarter the peppers lengthwise. Remove the stems and seeds. Cut small slits into the ends of the pieces to make them lie flat. Place pepper pieces, cut sides down, on a foil-lined baking sheet. Bake in a 425° oven for 20 to 25 minutes or until skins are bubbly and brown. Immediately place pepper pieces in a clean brown paper bag. Close bag tightly; cool.

- Meanwhile, cook broccoli in a covered medium saucepan in a small amount of boiling water for 5 minutes; drain well.

- Peel the cooled pepper pieces with a sharp knife. Cut lengthwise into ½-inch-wide strips; cut strips crosswise in half. Combine pepper strips, broccoli, tomatoes, and hearts of palm in a large bowl.

- For marinade, add the oil, parsley, water, lemon juice, garlic, basil, salt, and ground pepper to the Tupperware® Quick Shake® container. Apply seal and cap; shake well. Pour marinade over pepper mixture. Toss lightly to coat. Cover and chill for 4 to 24 hours, stirring occasionally.

- To serve, line salad plates with lettuce leaves. Divide pepper mixture among the plates. Makes 4 to 6 servings.

Vegetable Salad with Green Onion Dressing

Per serving:
118 cal. (39% from fat), 5 g pro., 15 g carbo., 6 g fat,
5 mg cholesterol, 5 g dietary fiber, 159 mg sodium.

Preparation time:
20 minutes

Chilling time:
4 hours

This creamy vegetable toss makes a light alternative to potato salad. For just-picked freshness, look for the cauliflower, summer squash, sweet pepper, and radishes at your local farmers' market.

2	cups cauliflower flowerets and/or broccoli flowerets
1	small yellow summer squash or zucchini, halved lengthwise and thinly sliced (1½ cups)
1	large red, yellow, or green sweet pepper, cut into bite-size strips
1	cup sliced radishes
1	cup frozen peas
½	cup Green Onion Dressing (see recipe at right)

- Combine cauliflower and/or broccoli flowerets, summer squash or zucchini, sweet pepper strips, radishes, and peas in a large bowl. Pour Green Onion Dressing over vegetables. Toss lightly to coat. Cover and chill for 4 to 12 hours. Makes 4 to 6 servings.

Green Onion Dressing: Combine ½ cup coarsely chopped *green onions*, ¼ cup *mayonnaise*, 1 tablespoon *white wine vinegar* or *white vinegar*, 1 tablespoon *Dijon-style mustard*, ¼ teaspoon *pepper*, and 1 clove *garlic*, halved, in a blender container or food processor bowl. Cover and blend or process until onion is finely chopped. Transfer the dressing to a small bowl. Stir in one 8-ounce carton *plain yogurt*. Cover and store in the refrigerator for up to 1 week. Makes about 1¼ cups (ten 2-tablespoon servings).

Warm Salad of Asparagus and Greens

Per serving:
150 cal. (60% from fat), 5 g pro., 11 g carbo., 11 g fat,
13 mg cholesterol, 3 g dietary fiber, 218 mg sodium.

**Preparation time:
25 minutes**

Frilly-leaved kale adds a cabbagelike flavor and firm texture to this tasty sweet-and-sour salad.

2   cups asparagus, cut into 2-inch pieces

4   slices bacon, cut into 1-inch pieces

1   small onion, sliced into rings

2   tablespoons vinegar

1   tablespoon sugar

½   teaspoon dried fines herbes, crushed

⅛   teaspoon salt

1   cup torn Bibb or Boston lettuce

1   cup torn kale or 1½ cups torn sorrel

1   tomato, chopped

• Cook asparagus in a covered small saucepan in a small amount of boiling water for 7 to 9 minutes or until just tender. Drain asparagus well.

• Meanwhile, cook bacon in a medium saucepan until crisp, stirring frequently. Drain bacon on paper towels, reserving *2 tablespoons* drippings in saucepan. Set bacon aside. Cook onion in drippings until tender.

• To serve, stir vinegar, sugar, fines herbes, and salt into onion and drippings in saucepan. Remove from heat. Stir in asparagus, bacon, lettuce, kale or sorrel, and tomato; toss lightly to coat. Makes 4 servings.

Quick-Cooked Vegetables

Need cooked vegetables for a salad in a hurry? No problem—micro-cook them in the Tupperware® Meals in Minutes™ microsteamer. First, wash, trim, and peel the fresh vegetables as necessary. Cut them into pieces, if specified. Arrange the vegetable pieces in the colander. Add ½ cup *water* to the dish. Place the colander in the dish. Cover and cook on 100% power (high) for the time shown or until the vegetables are crisp-tender, stirring or rearranging once.

Vegetables	Amount	Cooking Time
Asparagus spears	10 medium	3 to 4 minutes
Broccoli spears	6 ounces	4 to 6 minutes
Carrots, ¼-inch slices	1½ cups	5 to 6 minutes
Cauliflower flowerets	1½ cups	3½ to 4½ minutes
Pea pods	4 ounces	2 to 3 minutes
Peppers	1½ cups	3 to 5 minutes
Potatoes, quartered	2 small	7 to 8 minutes
Zucchini or yellow summer squash, cut into ¼-inch-thick slices	1½ cups	3 to 4 minutes

Summer Fruit Salad

Per serving:
193 cal. (42% from fat), 1 g pro., 29 g carbo., 10 g fat,
0 mg cholesterol, 2 g dietary fiber, 13 mg sodium.

Preparation time:
10 minutes

Chilling time:
2 hours

Assembling time:
10 minutes

Show off some glorious summer fruits flavored with a honey-lime and poppy seed dressing.

2   tablespoons honey

¼   teaspoon finely shredded lime peel

1   tablespoon lime juice

¼   cup salad oil

¼   teaspoon poppy seed

¼   of a medium honeydew melon

2   peeled peaches or 2 nectarines, cut into thin wedges (2 cups)

2   plums, cut into thin wedges (1 cup)

½   cup seedless red or green grapes, halved

¼   of a small cantaloupe

- Combine honey, lime peel, and lime juice in a small mixing bowl. Beat with an electric mixer on medium speed, adding salad oil to honey mixture in a thin steady stream. Continue beating until mixture is thick. Beat in poppy seed. Cover and chill 2 to 24 hours.

- Scoop melon balls from honeydew melon following the instructions in the tip on page 45. Combine melon balls, peaches or nectarines, plums, and grapes in the Tupperware® 6-cup serving bowl. Cut cantaloupe with shell-shaped melon baller or cut into very thin strips. Add to the fruit mixture. Drizzle dressing over all the fruit. Toss fruit lightly to mix. If desired, garnish with grape leaves. Makes 6 servings.

Ratatouille-Style Salad

Per serving:
105 cal. (65% from fat), 2 g pro., 8 g carbo., 8 g fat,
0 mg cholesterol, 2 g dietary fiber, 227 mg sodium.

Preparation time:
20 minutes

Chilling time:
4 hours

Standing time:
30 minutes

This salad's country-fresh flavor teams especially well with a grilled entrée.

2   small zucchini, halved lengthwise and cut into ½-inch-thick pieces

½   cup chopped onion

¼   cup chopped yellow sweet pepper

¼   cup chopped red sweet pepper

2   tablespoons olive oil or salad oil

1   cup chopped tomato

⅓   cup sliced pitted ripe olives

4   teaspoons snipped fresh basil or 1¼ teaspoons dried basil, crushed

¼   teaspoon salt

¼   teaspoon ground black pepper

- Cook zucchini, onion, yellow pepper, and red pepper in a medium saucepan in hot oil for 5 to 8 minutes or until just tender. Transfer mixture to a medium bowl. Stir in chopped tomato, sliced olives, basil, salt, and black pepper. Cover and chill for 4 to 24 hours.

- To serve, let salad stand at room temperature about 30 minutes. Makes 4 to 6 servings.

Summer Fruit Salad

Julienne Vegetable Salad

Per serving:
174 cal. (80% from fat), 3 g pro., 6 g carbo., 16 g fat, 14 mg cholesterol, 2 g dietary fiber, 255 mg sodium.

Preparation time: 30 minutes

Chilling time: 4 hours

The Parmesan-Dijon dressing also makes a wonderful party dip for vegetables, such as sweet pepper wedges, cucumber spears, and carrot sticks.

1½ cups water

1 medium zucchini, cut into julienne strips

2 stalks celery, cut into julienne strips

2 medium carrots, cut into julienne strips

1 red or green sweet pepper, cut into julienne strips

2 tablespoons sliced green onions

½ cup mayonnaise

¼ cup grated Parmesan cheese

2 teaspoons Dijon-style mustard

¼ teaspoon garlic powder

- Combine water, zucchini, celery, carrots, red or green pepper, and green onions in a medium saucepan. Cover and bring to boiling. Reduce heat; simmer about 3 minutes or until vegetables are just crisp-tender. Drain vegetables. Transfer to a large bowl; set aside.

- For dressing, combine mayonnaise, Parmesan cheese, mustard, and garlic powder in a small bowl. Pour dressing over vegetable mixture. Toss lightly to coat. Cover; chill for 4 to 24 hours. Makes 6 to 8 servings.

Today's Caesar Salad

Per serving:
151 cal. (68% from fat), 6 g pro., 6 g carbo., 12 g fat, 39 mg cholesterol, 1 g dietary fiber, 269 mg sodium.

Preparation time: 15 minutes

Chilling time: 2 hours

Our updated version of Caesar salad features a cooked egg dressing instead of the traditional uncooked dressing— a potential food hazard.

1 egg

⅓ cup chicken broth

3 anchovy fillets

3 tablespoons olive oil

2 tablespoons lemon juice

Few dashes white wine Worcestershire sauce

1 clove garlic, halved

10 cups torn romaine

½ cup Parmesan Croutons (see recipe, page 91) or purchased garlic croutons

¼ cup grated Parmesan cheese

Whole black peppercorns

- For dressing, combine egg, chicken broth, anchovy fillets, olive oil, lemon juice, and Worcestershire sauce in a blender container or food processor bowl. Cover and blend or process until smooth. Transfer dressing to a small saucepan. Cook and stir dressing over low heat for 8 to 10 minutes or until thickened. *Do not boil.* Transfer to a bowl. Cover and chill for 2 to 24 hours.

- To serve, rub the inside of a wooden salad bowl with the cut sides of the garlic clove; discard garlic clove. Add romaine, croutons, and Parmesan cheese to the salad bowl. Pour dressing over salad. Toss lightly to coat. Arrange mixture on 6 salad plates. Grind peppercorns over each serving. Makes 6 servings.

Classic
Potato Salad

Per serving:
282 cal. (66% from fat), 5 g pro., 19 g carbo., 21 g fat,
120 mg cholesterol, 2 g dietary fiber, 336 mg sodium.

Preparation time:
45 minutes

Chilling time:
6 hours

"Just like my Mom's" is the best way to describe this prized salad.

6   medium potatoes
    (2 pounds)

1¼ cups mayonnaise

1   tablespoon prepared
    mustard (optional)

½   teaspoon salt

¼   teaspoon pepper

1   cup thinly sliced celery

½   cup chopped onion

½   cup chopped sweet
    pickle or sweet pickle
    relish

6   hard-cooked eggs,
    coarsely chopped

    Lettuce leaves

    Paprika (optional)

- Cook potatoes in a covered saucepan in boiling water for 20 to 25 minutes or until just tender; drain well. Cool slightly. Peel and cube potatoes.

- Meanwhile, stir together mayonnaise, mustard (if desired), salt, and pepper in a large bowl.

- Stir in celery, onion, and sweet pickle or pickle relish. Add cooked potatoes and hard-cooked eggs. Toss lightly to coat. Cover and chill for 6 to 24 hours.

- To serve, line a large bowl with lettuce leaves. Spoon the potato salad into the lettuce-lined bowl. If desired, sprinkle with paprika. Makes 12 servings.

Perfect Potato Salad

The secret to making a delightfully creamy, yet chunky, potato salad is to use a variety that will hold its shape. Thin-skinned round reds or whites are a good choice for potato salad because they have a firm, waxy texture and won't fall apart when boiled. Mealy, thick-skinned potatoes, such as russets, are better for baking and mashing.

Finishing
Touches

Enhance your salad combinations with one of these special accents. Use Raspberry-Mint Vinegar to marinate vegetables, toss Parmesan Croutons with an assortment of greens, or drizzle Orange-Poppy Seed Oil-Free Dressing over fruit. Any of these crowning touches is sure to make your salads extraordinary.

Raspberry-Mint Vinegar, Herb Vinegars,
and Dill and Chive Dressing
(See recipes, pages 86–87.)

Herb Vinegar

Per serving:
2 cal. (2% from fat), 0 g pro., 1 g carbo., 0 g fat,
0 mg cholesterol, 0 g dietary fiber, 5 mg sodium.

Preparation time:
10 minutes

Standing time:
2 weeks

Take your choice of basil, tarragon, oregano, thyme, mint, rosemary, dill, or chervil when you make this herb-flavored wine vinegar. Then use it just as you would other vinegars.

½ cup tightly packed fresh herb leaves

2 cups white wine vinegar

- Wash desired herb leaves; pat dry with paper towels. Combine herb and vinegar in a small stainless steel or enamel saucepan. Bring *almost* to boiling. Remove from heat and loosely cover; cool. Pour mixture into a clean 1-quart jar. Cover the jar tightly with a nonmetallic lid. Let stand in a cool, dark place for 2 weeks.

- Line a colander with several layers of 100% cotton cheesecloth. Pour the vinegar mixture through the colander and let it drain into a bowl. Discard herb leaves. Pour the strained vinegar into a clean 1½-pint bottle or jar or the Tupperware® Modular Mates® Round 3 container. If desired, add an additional sprig of fresh herb to the bottle. Cover the bottle with a nonmetallic lid or seal the container. Store in a cool, dark place for up to 6 months. Makes about 32 (1-tablespoon) servings.

Note: Basil and tarragon vinegars are pictured on pages 84–85.

Raspberry-Mint Vinegar

Per serving:
9 cal. (1% from fat), 0 g pro., 2 g carbo., 0 g fat,
0 mg cholesterol, 0 g dietary fiber, 0 mg sodium.

Preparation time:
15 minutes

Standing time:
1 week

Combine equal amounts of this delicate, fruit-flavored vinegar with a mild salad oil to serve over your favorite mixed greens. If you have a few fresh raspberries on hand, sprinkle them on top.

2 teaspoons dried mint, crushed, or four 3- to 4-inch fresh mint sprigs

½ of a 12-ounce package lightly sweetened frozen red raspberries or 1½ cups fresh raspberries

2 cups cider vinegar

1 cup dry red wine

- Place the mint in a clean 1-quart jar. Set the jar aside. Thaw the raspberries, if frozen. (Or, rinse the fresh raspberries thoroughly with cold water and drain well.) Bring the raspberries, vinegar, and wine to boiling in a stainless steel or enamel saucepan. Boil the mixture gently, uncovered, for 3 minutes.

- Pour the hot mixture over the mint in the jar; let cool uncovered. Cover and let stand in a cool, dark place for 1 week.

- Line a colander with several layers of 100% cotton cheesecloth or a cup-shaped coffee filter. Pour the mixture through the colander and let it drain into a bowl. Transfer the strained liquid to a clean 1½-pint bottle or jar or the Tupperware Modular Mates Round 4 container. Cover tightly with a nonmetallic lid or seal the container. Store in the refrigerator for up to 6 months. Makes 48 (1-tablespoon) servings.

Note: Pictured on page 84.

Dill and Chive Dressing

Per serving:
57 cal. (93% from fat), 0 g pro., 1 g carbo., 6 g fat,
3 mg cholesterol, 0 g dietary fiber, 71 mg sodium.

**Preparation time:
10 minutes**

This rich and creamy dressing has a delightfully tangy flavor. As a seasoning option, try substituting 1 tablespoon fresh snipped dillweed for the 1 teaspoon dried dillweed.

½ cup dairy sour cream

2 tablespoons white wine vinegar

1 teaspoon sugar

1 teaspoon dried dillweed

½ teaspoon salt

½ teaspoon dry mustard

1 small clove garlic, minced

⅓ cup salad oil

2 tablespoons snipped chives

- Combine sour cream, vinegar, sugar, dillweed, salt, dry mustard, and garlic in a blender container or food processor bowl. Cover; blend or process for 5 seconds.

- Through the opening in the lid or with the lid ajar, and with blender or processor on slow speed, gradually add salad oil in a thin stream. (When necessary, stop blender or processor and scrape sides.) Stir in chives.

- Spoon into a small bowl or the Tupperware® Modular Mates® Oval 1 container. Cover the bowl or seal the container; refrigerate for up to 1 week. Stir before serving. Makes about 16 (1-tablespoon) servings.

Note: Pictured on page 85.

Green Goddess Dressing

Per serving:
45 cal. (91% from fat), 0 g pro., 1 g carbo., 5 g fat,
5 mg cholesterol, 0 g dietary fiber, 37 mg sodium.

**Preparation time:
10 minutes**

If you want to cut back on calories and fat, use nonfat or reduced-calorie mayonnaise for the regular mayonnaise and low-fat yogurt instead of the sour cream or plain yogurt.

¾ cup packed parsley leaves

⅓ cup mayonnaise

⅓ cup dairy sour cream or plain yogurt

1 green onion, cut up

1 tablespoon vinegar

1 teaspoon anchovy paste or 1 anchovy fillet, cut up

¼ teaspoon dried basil, crushed

⅛ teaspoon garlic powder

⅛ teaspoon dried tarragon, crushed

1 to 2 tablespoons milk

- Combine parsley, mayonnaise, sour cream or yogurt, green onion, vinegar, anchovy paste, basil, garlic powder, and tarragon in a blender container or food processor bowl. Cover and blend or process until the mixture is smooth.

- Spoon into a small bowl or the Tupperware Modular Mates Round 2 container. Cover the bowl or seal the container; refrigerate for up to 2 weeks. Before serving, stir in milk to make dressing the desired consistency. Makes about 16 (1-tablespoon) servings.

Sun-Dried Tomato Vinaigrette

Per serving:
29 cal. (75% from fat), 0 g pro., 2 g carbo., 3 g fat,
0 mg cholesterol, 0 g dietary fiber, 45 mg sodium.

Preparation time:
10 minutes

Sun-dried tomatoes add a mildly sweet, rich flavor to this sophisticated dressing. Look for dried tomato halves or slices packed in oil and snip them into small pieces or purchase tomato bits packed in oil.

¼ cup vinegar

¼ cup snipped sun-dried tomatoes (oil pack)

2 tablespoons oil from sun-dried tomatoes or olive oil

2 tablespoons water

1 tablespoon snipped fresh oregano or tarragon or 1 teaspoon dried oregano or tarragon, crushed

1 tablespoon Dijon-style mustard

1 teaspoon sugar

- Add vinegar, snipped tomatoes, oil, water, oregano or tarragon, mustard, and sugar to the Tupperware® Quick Shake® container. Apply seal and cap; shake well.

- Store in the refrigerator for up to 1 week. Shake well before serving. Makes about 12 (1-tablespoon) servings.

Tofu Salad Dressing

Per serving:
14 cal. (40% from fat), 1 g pro., 1 g carbo., 1 g fat,
0 mg cholesterol, 0 g dietary fiber, 22 mg sodium.

Preparation time:
10 minutes

Chilling time:
2 hours

Although tofu itself is almost tasteless, it easily absorbs other flavors. In this tasty and nutritious dressing, it takes on the tangy flavors of buttermilk and vinegar, the pungent flavor of dry mustard, and the sweet, fragrant flavor of Italian herb seasoning.

4 ounces soft tofu (fresh bean curd), cubed

⅓ cup buttermilk

2 tablespoons vinegar

½ teaspoon dried Italian herb seasoning, crushed

¼ teaspoon dry mustard

1 small clove garlic, minced

Dash salt

Dash pepper

¼ teaspoon celery seed

- Combine tofu, buttermilk, vinegar, Italian herb seasoning, dry mustard, garlic, salt, and pepper in a blender container or food processor bowl. Cover and blend or process until smooth. Stir in celery seed.

- Spoon into a small bowl or the Tupperware Modular Mates® Round 1 container. Cover the bowl or seal the container and chill for 2 to 24 hours. Makes about 10 (1-tablespoon) servings.

Low-Calorie Thousand Island Dressing

Per serving:
17 cal. (51% from fat), 0 g pro., 2 g carbo., 1 g fat,
1 mg cholesterol, 0 g dietary fiber, 59 mg sodium.

Preparation time:
10 minutes

You'll save 50 calories and 7 grams of fat per table-spoon when you use this slimmed-down version of Thousand Island dressing.

⅓ cup plain low-fat yogurt

2 tablespoons reduced-calorie mayonnaise

2 tablespoons chili sauce

1 tablespoon finely chopped green or red sweet pepper

1 tablespoon finely chopped onion

1 tablespoon skim milk

½ teaspoon paprika

1 hard-cooked egg white, finely chopped (optional)

• Stir together the yogurt, mayonnaise, and chili sauce in a small bowl. Stir in the chopped pepper, onion, skim milk, paprika, and, if desired, the chopped egg white.

• Spoon into a small bowl or the Tupperware® Modular Mates® Round 1 container. Cover the bowl or seal the container and store in the refrigerator for up to 1 week. Makes about 12 (1-tablespoon) servings.

Orange-Poppy Seed Oil-Free Dressing

Per serving:
18 cal. (3% from fat), 0 g pro., 5 g carbo., 0 g fat,
0 mg cholesterol, 0 g dietary fiber, 0 mg sodium.

Preparation time:
10 minutes

Chilling time:
3 hours

Toss this honey-sweetened dressing with sliced fresh apples, pears, or peaches and torn greens. Or drizzle it over orange sections.

¼ teaspoon finely shredded orange peel

⅓ cup orange juice

1 tablespoon powdered fruit pectin

1 tablespoon honey

¼ teaspoon poppy seed

• Stir together orange peel, orange juice, fruit pectin, honey, and poppy seed in a small bowl. Cover and refrigerate at least 3 hours before using.

• To store, transfer dressing to the Tupperware Quick Shake® container. Apply seal and cap. Store in the refrigerator for up to 3 days. Shake dressing before serving. Makes about 8 (1-tablespoon) servings.

Iceberg Options

Of all the salad greens, iceberg lettuce probably is the most popular. That's not surprising because it tastes great with many kinds of dressings and is easy to serve. Tearing iceberg lettuce into bite-size pieces is the traditional way to serve it, but for a little variety, here are some other shapes to try.

Wedges: Cut a head in half. Place each half, cut side down, on a cutting board. Then cut each half lengthwise into thirds.
Rafts: Cut a head crosswise into 1-inch-thick slices.
Chunks: Make rafts. Cut each raft into bite-size chunks.
Shredded: Cut a head in half. Place each half, cut side down, on a cutting board. Cut crosswise into long, coarse shreds.

Low-Calorie Italian Dressing

Per serving:
2 cal. (3% from fat), 0 g pro., 0 g carbo., 0 g fat,
0 mg cholesterol, 0 g dietary fiber, 43 mg sodium.

Preparation time:
10 minutes

Chilling time:
8 hours

With this oil-free dressing you can enjoy the tangy herb flavor of Italian dressing without all the fat and calories. A 1-tablespoon serving has less than ½ gram of fat and only 2 calories.

2   tablespoons liquid fruit pectin

2   tablespoons finely chopped onion

¼   teaspoon garlic salt

¼   teaspoon dried basil, crushed

⅛   teaspoon dried oregano, crushed

⅛   teaspoon crushed red pepper

2   tablespoons cider vinegar

- Combine fruit pectin, onion, garlic salt, basil, oregano, and crushed red pepper in a small bowl. Stir in ½ cup *water* and cider vinegar. Cover and refrigerate for 8 hours or overnight before using.

- To store, transfer dressing to the Tupperware® Quick Shake® container. Apply seal and cap. Store in the refrigerator for up to 3 days. Shake dressing before serving. Makes about 10 (1-tablespoon) servings.

Parmesan Croutons

Per serving:
55 cal. (57% from fat), 1 g pro., 5 g carbo., 3 g fat,
1 mg cholesterol, 0 g dietary fiber, 99 mg sodium.

Preparation time:
25 minutes

Be sure to make a double batch. You'll find it hard to keep from snitching these flavorful salad toppers as a snack.

¼   cup margarine or butter

3   tablespoons grated Parmesan cheese

⅛   teaspoon garlic powder

½   teaspoon dried Italian herb seasoning, crushed (optional)

4   ½-inch-thick slices French bread, cut into ¾-inch squares

- Melt margarine or butter in a large skillet. Remove from heat. Stir in Parmesan cheese, garlic powder, and, if desired, Italian herb seasoning. Add bread cubes, stirring until the cubes are coated.

- Spread bread cubes in a single layer in a shallow baking pan. Bake in a 300° oven for 10 minutes; stir. Continue baking about 5 minutes more or until bread cubes are dry and crisp. Cool completely before using.

- To store croutons, place them in a bowl or the Tupperware One Touch™ Junior 5-cup canister. Cover bowl tightly or seal the canister; store for up to 1 week. Makes 16 (2-tablespoon) servings.

Dill Croutons: Prepare as above, *except* omit the Parmesan cheese, garlic powder, and Italian herb seasoning. Stir 1 teaspoon *dried dillweed* into the melted margarine or butter. (The nutrition information per serving is the same as Parmesan Croutons *except:* 50 cal. [56% from fat], 0 mg cholesterol, 78 mg sodium.)

Pumpernickel Croutons: Prepare as above, *except* substitute 4 slices *pumpernickel bread* for the French bread. Omit the Parmesan cheese, garlic powder, and Italian herb seasoning. Stir ¼ teaspoon *onion powder* into the melted margarine or butter. (The nutrition information per serving is the same as Parmesan Croutons *except:* 46 cal. [60% from fat], 4 g carbo., 0 mg cholesterol, 78 mg sodium.)

Creamy Herb Dressing

Per serving:
55 cal. (89% from fat), 1 g pro., 1 g carbo., 6 g fat, 6 mg cholesterol, 0 g dietary fiber, 67 mg sodium.

Preparation time: 10 minutes

Keep this creamy combo on hand in a Tupperware® Modular Mates® Round 1 container to serve over tossed vegetable salads.

¼	cup loosely packed parsley leaves or fresh basil leaves
¼	cup mayonnaise
¼	cup dairy sour cream
2	tablespoons thinly sliced green onions
2	teaspoons lemon juice
2	teaspoons Dijon-style mustard

- Combine parsley or basil leaves, mayonnaise, sour cream, green onions, lemon juice, and mustard in a blender container or food processor bowl. Cover and blend or process until smooth.

- Spoon the dressing into a small bowl or the Tupperware Modular Mates Round 1 container. Cover the bowl or seal the container and store in the refrigerator for up to 1 week. Makes about 10 (1-tablespoon) servings.

Low-Calorie Tomato-Basil Vinaigrette

Per serving:
5 cal. (3% from fat), 0 g pro., 1 g carbo., 0 g fat, 0 mg cholesterol, 0 g dietary fiber, 65 mg sodium.

Preparation time: 10 minutes

This dressing has a robust flavor and temptingly good looks. It lacks only some fat and calories.

⅔	cup tomato sauce
¼	cup red wine vinegar
1	tablespoon snipped fresh basil or 1 teaspoon dried basil, crushed
1	teaspoon sugar
½	teaspoon Worcestershire sauce
¼	teaspoon prepared horseradish

- Add the tomato sauce, red wine vinegar, basil, sugar, Worcestershire sauce, horseradish, and 1 tablespoon *water* to the Tupperware Quick Shake® container. Apply seal and cap; shake mixture well.

- Refrigerate for up to 1 week. Shake well before serving. Makes about 16 (1-tablespoon) servings.

Creamy Cucumber Salad Dressing

Per serving:
45 cal. (93% from fat), 0 g pro., 1 g carbo., 5 g fat, 5 mg cholesterol, 0 g dietary fiber, 30 mg sodium.

Preparation time: 10 minutes

Omitting the milk from this dressing transforms it into a terrific vegetable dip. Serve the dip with an assortment of vegetable dippers in the Tupperware Serving Center.®

½	cup mayonnaise
½	cup dairy sour cream
2	tablespoons snipped chives or thinly sliced green onions
¾	cup peeled, seeded, and finely chopped cucumber
2	tablespoons to ¼ cup milk

- Stir together mayonnaise, sour cream, and chives or green onions in a small bowl. Stir in the chopped cucumber. Stir in milk to make the dressing the desired consistency.

- Spoon the dressing into a bowl or the Tupperware Modular Mates Oval 1 container. Cover the bowl or seal the container and store in the refrigerator for up to 1 week. Makes about 24 (1-tablespoon) servings.

Basic Vinaigrette

Per serving:
54 cal. (98% from fat), 0 g pro., 0 g carbo., 6 g fat,
0 mg cholesterol, 0 g dietary fiber, 2 mg sodium.

**Preparation time:
10 minutes**

Nothing can top a well-seasoned vinaigrette for dressing up crisp greens, vegetables, or fruits. Pick your favorite among these five delightful variations.

⅓ cup salad oil

⅓ cup white wine vinegar or vinegar

1 tablespoon sugar (optional)

2 teaspoons snipped fresh thyme or oregano or ½ teaspoon dried thyme or oregano, crushed

½ teaspoon paprika

¼ teaspoon dry mustard or 1 teaspoon Dijon-style mustard

⅛ teaspoon pepper

- Add oil, vinegar, sugar (if desired), thyme or oregano, paprika, mustard, and pepper to the Tupperware® Quick Shake® container. Apply seal and cap; shake well. Refrigerate for up to 2 weeks. Shake well before serving. Makes 12 (1-tablespoon) servings.

Red Wine Vinaigrette: Prepare as above, *except* reduce vinegar to *3 tablespoons.* Use half thyme and half oregano. Add 2 tablespoons *dry red wine* and 1 clove *garlic,* minced. (The nutrition information per serving is the same as Basic Vinaigrette *except:* 56 cal. [94% from fat].)

Italian Vinaigrette: Prepare as above, *except* use only oregano. Add 2 tablespoons grated *Parmesan cheese,* ¼ teaspoon *celery seed,* and 1 clove *garlic,* minced. (The nutrition information per serving is the same as Basic Vinaigrette *except:* 60 cal. [94% from fat], 1 mg cholesterol, 22 mg sodium.)

Citrus and Poppy Seed Vinaigrette: Prepare as above, *except* substitute *lemon juice* or *lime juice* for the vinegar and *honey* for the sugar. Omit herb. Add 1 teaspoon *poppy seed.* (The nutrition information per serving is the same as Basic Vinaigrette *except:* 61 cal. [86% from fat], 2 g carbo., 0 mg sodium.)

Ginger Vinaigrette: Prepare as above, *except* omit the herb and mustard. Add 1 teaspoon grated *gingerroot.* (The nutrition information per serving is the same as Basic Vinaigrette *except:* 57 cal. [94% from fat], 1 g carbo., 3 mg sodium.)

Fresh Herb Hints

Often what makes a salad or salad dressing truly distinctive is the added flavor of fresh herbs. You don't really need a recipe to use them. Just snip a few sprigs of your favorite herb and add them to a tossed salad. To get the most from the herbs you use:

Buy fresh herbs in small quantities because they will last only a few days in the refrigerator.

To cut herbs into fine pieces, place the sprigs in a 1-cup measuring cup and snip with kitchen shears.

To substitute most fresh herbs for dried, triple the amount of dried herb called for. Or, if you can't get a particular fresh herb and want to use dried, use about one-third of the amount of fresh herb called for. (Don't forget to crush the dried herbs before adding them to mixtures to release more of their flavor.)

Index

Index *(continued)*

So you can keep track of what you eat, each recipe in this book lists the nutrition values for one serving. Here's how we made our analyses.

When a recipe gives a choice of ingredients (such as Swiss or cheddar cheese), we used the first choice in our analysis.

Ingredients listed as optional were omitted from our calculations.

Finally, we rounded all values to the nearest whole number.